# one pan feasts

# one pan feasts

Easy entertaining for
any occasion

**Dominic Franks**

# Cont

# ents

# Introduction

## Where It All Started

Welcome to my second book and the follow-up to *Upside Down Cooking*. When I was thinking about ideas for this cookbook, I wanted it to be about my love of cooking simple, accessible food. Food that can be shared and enjoyed by everyone, whether they are a first-time cook or confident in the kitchen. I grew up in the '70s and '80s in London in a family where food was the centre of every occasion. Mum, along with my grandmas, instilled the art of creating feasts to share with family and friends. We'd indulge, but it was always more about generosity than gluttony.

My parents would often host dinner parties, and this being the height of the '80s, we're talking about professional middle-class hosting. A G&T on arrival, four courses, including cheese, and a different wine for each course, not forgetting the ubiquitous hostess trolley, and Bendicks chocolate mints served with real coffee to finish. All the men wore blazers and the women long, flowing dresses, or later on, sparkly, patterned knitwear with shoulder pads. The fug of Dior's Poison would be almost as overpowering as the intoxicating aromas coming from the kitchen.

As kids, we were allowed to say hello to guests as they arrived, but then had to make ourselves scarce, and would take ourselves off to bed in true Von Trapp family reluctance. I remember sneaking downstairs as each course passed from the kitchen to the dining room, admiring what was about to be served, then I'd listen out for the ooohs and aaahs from the guests. The next morning, I'd slip into the dining room to soak in the leftover atmosphere, the air still heavy with the scent of roasted meats, whisky, and Auntie Fran's Silk Cuts.

As I grew older, Mum would let me serve the guests. A soup course was always tricky, but for the main course, I would start with the side dishes, announcing each one with theatrical flair to squeals of delight from the wives – lapping up the praise as though I had cooked the food.

These memorable dinners may have been when my love for hosting and celebrating began, or it could have been the many Sunday spreads that Mum used to make for parties at our house. Birthdays, anniversaries, and numerous Jewish festivals were all marked by the moving of sofas to be replaced by tables draped with giant bedsheets and then generously dressed with the most incredible plates of food. Mountains of bagels, ribbons of smoked salmon, little glass bowls filled with cream cheese or egg and onion, chopped liver, or taramasalata. Fried fish balls were also popular: little round balls, large flat salmon balls, and gefilte fish with a small slice of carrot on top. And there was always Mum's speciality, quiche. Each event was a feast for the eyes as well as the belly.

## My Love of One-Pan Feasts

A feast for me is not necessarily a table groaning with food, like some kind of bacchanalian celebration, although it can be exactly that if you so desire. Feasts are about enjoying food in a way that I feel we've lost somewhat in our health- and fitness-obsessed lives. We've forgotten how to enjoy good food for how it tastes and how it satisfies the soul. But, importantly, how to prepare a feast in a way that lets the cook enjoy the party too, and feel the satisfaction of inviting guests to the table and sharing the joy of feasting.

Of course I love nothing more than hosting, but none of us want to deal with the mountains of washing up, stress, and faff that it entails. In my opinion, one-pan feasting is the answer!

There's no better way to celebrate than with a meal made in a single pan – which is why the recipes in this book are made for one pan, pot, or tray, with upside-down creations, and a host of other ways to flip, feast, and enjoy feeding a crowd. I've designed the recipes in this book to make hosting easy, with simple dishes that can be prepped in advance and served up without a hassle, in a single pan. So you can get ahead for one-pan worknight suppers, Sunday lunch, Christmas dinner, and birthday brunches, and take part in the memories created at a dining table when you've lovingly made the meal.

## About My Book

I'm hoping that, like me and others across the world, you'll have already embraced the upside-down concept, but just in case you're new to it, let me explain. Upside-down cooking is the simple concept of layering ingredients on a single baking tray to build a dish in reverse. It's an idea that works brilliantly with one-pot dishes like tarts and pies: start with a drizzle of olive oil, honey, or sugar to help the cooking process, then top the baking tray with the "filling" ingredients, and complete it with a blanket of puff or shortcrust pastry on top. Once in the oven, the heat from the metal baking tray below and the cover of the pastry on top, cook the filling to glorious perfection. When baked, you then have the theatrics of flipping the tart or pie over to reveal the finished, glorious dish.

The possibilities are almost endless: from sweet and savoury traybakes, to one-pan, weeknight meals and seasonal treats – wherever your imagination and the ingredients in your fridge take you. I often ask guests who are coming to dinner what their favourite meal is, and then turn it into an upside-down version in tart or pie form; taking the essence of the dish and layering it under pastry. I love to take a classic recipe and ponder how it could work in layers, finally adapting it into an upside-down version. Once you have the technique figured out, you can get creative with your own inventions too.

This book is packed full of my favourite one-pan and upside-down dishes for occasions to feast. Some are for seasonal celebrations, such as Christmas Day, Halloween, or Valentine's Day; while others focus on everyday feasts, like a simple, informal supper to enjoy with friends and family at home. You'll also find a chapter on dinner parties, with multiple-course meals that you'll be able to prepare in advance and enjoy with your guests. There are recipes for every kind of mealtime and occasion, from brunches and picnics to lunches and dinners. There are one-pot dishes for gatherings, large and small, and even mini feasts just for you – a little indulgent treat to spoil yourself. Feel free to follow these recipes to the letter, or use them to inspire your own creations. Whether you embrace the upside down, or simply enjoy the delights of one-pan cooking, I hope you will fill your eyes, hearts, and bellies with the ideas in this book. Happy feasting!

*Love, Dom x*

# Equipment & Ingredients

Simplicity is key when it comes to the way I like to cook, and that extends to the type of kitchen tools and ingredients I use. You're likely to have most of the equipment listed below but I thought I'd share with you some of my most loved and used items, the stuff that works and brings me success. The same goes for basic ingredients; there is nothing fancy here, but they are all essentials when it comes to my style of upside-down cooking.

### Baking Tray
The baking tray I use is the Nordic Ware Jelly Roll Pan from their Naturals range, which measures 38 x 27cm (15 x 10½in). It's aluminium, which is a great conductor of heat and perfect for even cooking. It also has shallow sides, making it easier to slide a spatula under the tart, or for putting a board on top for the flip. You don't want to be elbowing the sides of your baking tray out the way and ruining the shape of the tart, but equally you don't want a flat sheet with the risk of the tart sliding off.

### Baking Parchment
I would advise lining your baking tray with baking parchment, also known as greaseproof paper or baking paper, as it prevents the tarts and pies sticking to the tray and allows you to easily flip them over once baked. It also helps to keep the fillings of the larger pies in place, and once flipped over will ensure you can peel off the backing paper to reveal the pie without damaging or losing the top. A small amount of butter around the inside edge of the tray can also help to hold the baking parchment in place.

### Egg Wash
I always brush my pastry tarts and pies with beaten egg before they go into the oven. For an egg-free version, you can use a splash of milk or a milk alternative, or even a light vegetable oil. All give a beautifully bronzed pastry after baking.

### Food-safe Pencil
For many of the recipes, I suggest tracing around a plate or a template with a pencil. It also helps with knowing where to place the tart topping on the baking tray if you mark the outline of the tart on the baking parchment first. You should use a food-safe pencil or, failing that, draw on one side of the paper and flip it over, since most baking paper is transparent.

### Oils & Sweeteners
Depending on which recipe you're making, the first ingredient used in all my tarts and pies, sweet or savoury, is either olive oil or honey. A drizzle of oil or honey over the baking parchment-lined baking tray helps cook and add colour to your tart or pie, often creating a beautiful golden patina on the top and around the pastry edges. I use a good-quality olive oil for the savoury dishes (and sometimes butter). Runny honey is my preference for the sweet dishes, but this can be substituted for golden syrup, maple syrup, or agave.

### Pastry
The great thing about the baking tray recommended, above, is that it is the perfect fit for the ready-rolled pastry sheets I use. Here, in the UK, most large supermarkets stock ready-made sheets of pastry, including puff pastry, shortcrust, and filo, all of which can be found in the chiller cabinet. Some larger supermarkets also stock vegan and gluten-free versions, which are both perfectly good alternatives. I most often buy the ready-rolled puff pastry and the brand Jus-Rol makes a delicious all-butter one. It comes in a 35 x 23cm (14 x 9in) sheet. The shop-bought sheets of shortcrust pastry are the same size, while the filo comes in boxes of 7 or 12 sheets.

### Pastry Brush

This is a useful tool for brushing the egg wash over the pastry before baking to give it a golden glow. I prefer a silicone brush.

### Tape Measure & Templates

I want to avoid making this sound like a maths class, but I'm also keen to avoid waste, so most of my recipes for tarts and pies are based on the size of the ready-rolled puff pastry sheets that are readily available to buy (see opposite). The same goes for the shortcrust pastry, which is of a similar dimension.

For ease and to avoid leftovers, the pastry sheets can be divided into even-sized pieces with some simple maths. A tape measure is handy for this, but you can also draw around a baking tin, ramekin, cookie cutter, or bowl for the circular tarts and pies.

Most of the tarts and pies in this book fit into the following sizes (see the table, below) but remember that the pastry can stretch as you handle it so don't worry if they come out a little wonky or misshapen; you can always trim the pastry once it's placed on the baking tray.

### Tart & Pie Dimensions

The tart and pie recipes in this book come in the following sizes. All will fit on a sheet of shop-bought puff, shortcrust, or filo pastry.

| | |
|---|---|
| 2 rectangles: 17 x 23cm (6½ x 9in) | |
| 4 rectangles: 11 x 17cm (4½ x 6½in) | |
| 6 squares: 11 x 11cm (4½ x 4½in) | |
| 8 rectangles: 11 x 8.5cm (4½ x 3½in) | |
| 12 rectangles: 7.5 x 8.5cm (3 x 3½in) | |

# My Go-To Pastry Recipes

If you can't get hold of ready-made pastry easily or just fancy making your own, here are my foolproof recipes that always work for me. The pastry, once made, will keep in the fridge for up to 3 days or the freezer for 3 months, well wrapped.

## Simple "Ruff" Puff Pastry

**MAKES ABOUT 500G (1LB 2OZ)**

This recipe isn't quite as complicated or lengthy as making "real" puff pastry, but I think it tastes just as delicious and works well with my tarts and pies. Sure, it still takes a while because there are a few stages to master, but it delivers a wonderfully flaky, layered crust every time. It is inspired by my sister-in-law Mo's recipe, and she makes the best sausage rolls with it. It's definitely a lazy day project. Put the kettle on, do a few jobs around the house and come back to it every 20 minutes or so and by the end of the day, you'll have a stunning block of pastry ready to use as you wish.

250g (9oz) plain flour, plus extra for dusting
1 tsp fine sea salt
250g (9oz) frozen lightly salted butter (place
   in the freezer 24 hours prior to making),
   coarsely grated
roughly 150ml (5fl oz) chilled water

1  Sift the flour and salt into a large bowl. Rub the butter loosely into the flour with your fingertips – you should still be able to see flecks of butter. Make a well in the middle of the flour mixture and pour in about two-thirds of the chilled water, stirring with a clawed hand, until you have a firm, rough dough. Add extra water if the dough is too dry to bring it all together.

2  Flatten the dough out into a rough rectangle, wrap it in cling film and leave to rest for 20 minutes in the freezer.

3  Turn the dough out onto a lightly floured worktop, knead gently and form it into a smooth rectangle. Using a rolling pin, roll the dough in one direction, until three times the length, about 20 x 50cm (8 x 20in), with one of the short sides facing you. It should look marbled with butter.

4  Fold the top third down to the centre and the bottom third up, like a letter. Give the dough a quarter turn to the right and roll it out again to three times the length, the same size as before. Fold as before. Wrap the pastry in cling film and freeze for another 20 minutes before repeating this process twice more, turning the pastry a quarter turn to the right each time. The pastry is now ready to use or can be kept in the fridge for up to 3 days or stored in the freezer for 3 months.

## Classic Shortcrust Pastry

**MAKES ABOUT 400G (14OZ)**

I learnt to make pastry from Mum. When I was a kid, I used to spend hours propped up at the kitchen counter watching her make quiches and tarts, and they all started with a classic shortcrust pastry. Sure, she taught me about measurements and the ratio of fat to flour, but she also taught me not to worry about it all that much. A classic shortcrust is just a combination of three simple, inexpensive ingredients. If you want to throw in ground almonds as well as flour or grated Cheddar instead of some of the butter, then do it. Play with it... what's the worst that can happen? I loved watching Mum bring it all together in a bowl (or even in a food processor, which takes seconds) but most of all, of course, I loved what eventually came out of the oven. After all, anything wrapped in a gloriously golden, melt-in-the-mouth pastry must be good.

250g (9oz) plain flour
150g (5½oz) cold lightly salted butter, diced
1–2 tbsp chilled water

1   Sift the flour into a large bowl and rub in the butter with your fingertips until you have something resembling breadcrumbs. Keep your movements light and quick. Add 1–2 tablespoons of chilled water and bring it together into a ball of dough with your hands. You may need to add a little more water – the pastry should feel smooth and slightly dry and not too wet, just damp enough to leave the inside of the bowl clean.

2   Flatten the pastry slightly, wrap in cling film and pop it in the fridge for at least 30 minutes. The pastry is now ready to use or can be kept in the fridge for up to 3 days or stored in the freezer for 3 months.

**Note:** Shortcrust can also be made in a food processor. Place the flour and butter in first and whizz to the breadcrumb stage, then add the water and whizz again until a smooth ball of dough forms.

## Cheese & Herb Shortcrust Pastry
**MAKES ABOUT 600G (1LB 5OZ)**

This pastry is easy to make and versatile. A strong Cheddar works well, but you can easily swap it for another type of hard cheese, such as Parmesan, Gruyère or Red Leicester, each adding its own unique flavour to the pastry. You can also vary the herbs with dried ones working just as well as fresh – simply halve the quantity if using. The pastry can also be made in a food processor.

300g (10oz) plain flour
250g (9oz) cold lightly salted butter, diced
50g (1¾oz) strong Cheddar, finely grated
1 tsp chopped thyme leaves
1 tsp chopped rosemary leaves
1 tsp dried oregano
½ tsp mustard powder
roughly 2 tbsp chilled whole milk or water

1   Sift the flour into a large bowl and rub in the butter with your fingertips until you have something resembling breadcrumbs. Stir in the cheese, herbs, and mustard with a fork. Add half of the chilled milk or water and bring it together into a ball of dough with your hands. You may need to add a little more milk or water – the pastry should feel smooth and slightly dry and not too wet, just damp enough to leave the inside of the bowl clean.

2   Flatten the pastry slightly, wrap in cling film and pop it in the fridge for at least 30 minutes. The pastry is now ready to use or can be kept in the fridge or stored in the freezer (see Classic Shortcrust Pastry, left).

# Sauces & Condiments

These flavourful sauces and condiments add an extra dimension to my upside-down tarts and pies, and while versions of them can be shop-bought, it's always nice if you can find the time to prepare your own. They're all easy to make, and once you've tried homemade, it's hard to go back.

## Tomato & Olive Sauce
**MAKES ROUGHLY 300ML (10FL OZ)**

½ onion, finely chopped
drizzle of extra-virgin olive oil
2 garlic cloves, finely grated
1 tsp chopped fresh oregano
1 tsp dried oregano
60g (2oz) mixed green and black pitted olives, roughly chopped
2 x 400g (14oz) cans chopped tomatoes
300ml (10fl oz) vegetable stock
2 tbsp balsamic vinegar
1 tsp tomato paste
splash of dry white wine
pinch of sugar
salt and freshly ground black pepper

1   Sauté the onion in a little olive oil in a heavy-based saucepan on a medium heat for roughly 6 minutes, until softened. Stir frequently so the onion cooks evenly. Add the garlic and half of the fresh and all of the dried oregano and cook gently for another 4 minutes, or until the onion starts to colour. Stir in the chopped olives.

2   Pour in the canned tomatoes, then refill the cans with the stock and add to the pan to remove any tomatoey residue. Stir in the balsamic vinegar, tomato paste, white wine, and sugar, then season well with salt and pepper.

3   Allow the sauce to come to the boil, then turn the heat down to the lowest setting and let it gently bubble and simmer away for at least 2 hours, until thickened. It should reduce by half, if not more. Stir in the remaining fresh oregano at the end and leave to cool.

**Note:** This slow-cooked sauce is my go-to (with and without the olives). It works with many dishes, from dressing a simple bowl of pasta to spooning it on top of a pizza base, and serving it with meatballs. Once made, it can be kept in the fridge for up to 1 week or frozen for up to 1 month.

## White / Cheese Sauce
**MAKES ROUGHLY 500ML (16FL OZ)**

500ml (16fl oz) milk (I used skimmed but go with your choice)
50g (1¾oz) plain flour
50g (1¾oz) lightly salted butter
salt and freshly ground black pepper

1   Place a saucepan on a medium heat, pour in the milk, then add the flour and butter. Using a balloon whisk, gently whisk the sauce for about 6 minutes, until lusciously creamy and thickened.

2   Turn the heat to its lowest setting and cook the sauce for a further 5 minutes, whisking every so often to ensure it doesn't catch on the bottom. Stir in a little salt and pepper to taste. The sauce is now ready to use or turned into a cheese sauce (see below).

**Note:** This all-in-one method results in a classic white sauce, perfect for lasagne or fish pie, but you can pimp it up by adding your favourite cheeses. For a light, creamy sauce, stir in 100g (3½oz) cream cheese when the white sauce has finished cooking. For a stronger-tasting sauce, add 85g (3oz) grated strong Cheddar and stir until melted and combined.

# Red Onion Jam
**MAKES ROUGHLY 2 X 500G (1LB 2OZ) JARS**

3 tbsp olive oil
1kg (2¼lb) red onions, cut in half lengthways,
  then finely sliced
150g (5½oz) soft light brown sugar
150ml (5fl oz) red wine vinegar
100ml (3½fl oz) red wine
3 tbsp whisky
2 tbsp balsamic vinegar
salt and freshly ground black pepper

**1**  Place a large casserole or heavy-based
   saucepan on a low heat. Add the oil and
   the onions and cook gently for 30 minutes,
   stirring occasionally, until softened and
   starting to caramelize.

**2**  Add a third of the sugar and cook for another
   15 minutes, stirring regularly, then add
   the rest of the sugar and the remaining
   ingredients. Stir and season with salt and
   pepper, to taste. Continue to simmer on
   the lowest heat setting until the liquid has
   reduced, and the onions are dark and sticky.
   It should take 30–45 minutes, depending
   on the size of your pan, to become a thick
   onion jam.

**3**  Carefully ladle the jam into sterilized jars
   while it's still hot and seal with vinegar-proof
   lids. Leave the jam to cool.

**4**  Store in a cool, dry place and use within
   3 months. Keep in the fridge once opened
   and use within 2 weeks.

# Pesto
**MAKES ROUGHLY 250ML (9FL OZ)**

50g (1¾oz) pine nuts
1 bunch of fresh basil, including stalks,
  roughly 85g (3oz)
50g (1¾oz) Parmesan, finely grated
150ml (5½fl oz) extra-virgin olive oil
2 garlic cloves, peeled

**1**  Heat a small frying pan over a low heat.
   Add the pine nuts and toast, shaking the
   pan occasionally, until just golden (you want
   to avoid them burning). Tip the nuts into a
   bowl and leave to cool.

**2**  When cool, tip the nuts into a food processor
   with the basil, Parmesan, oil, and garlic and
   blitz until almost smooth. Use straight away
   or transfer the pesto to a lidded container
   (it will keep, covered, for up to 3 days in
   the fridge).

**Note:** You can replace the pine nuts with
pistachios or walnuts. Use rocket instead of basil
for a peppery flavour. A strong, crumbly Cheddar
also works well in place of the Parmesan.

# My No-Knead "Sourdough" Bread

While this bread isn't quick to make, it takes less time than regular sourdough, and tastes similar to the real thing. Rather than the traditional method of kneading the dough on a floured work top, the dough is stretched and folded while still in the bowl, then it is left to rest overnight to allow the flavour to develop. The impressive loaf makes a great accompaniment to the dips (see p48) in this book, as well as the main event in the Picnic Loaf (see p71) recipe. You can choose to make one large free-form, crusty loaf or bake it in a loaf tin, or form the dough into rolls for crisp-on-the-outside, soft-on-the-inside buns of joy. The dough can be made a day in advance and then baked in the morning when needed.

## INGREDIENTS

500g (1lb 2oz) strong white bread flour
100g (3½oz) rye or wholemeal flour
400ml (14fl oz) lukewarm water
7g packet (2¼ tsp) instant dried yeast
1 tsp salt (I use a flaky sea salt)
1 tsp extra virgin olive oil, plus extra
    for greasing

## YOU WILL NEED

26cm (10½in) diameter cast-iron casserole dish
    or heavy-based ovenproof pot with a lid
stand mixer with a dough hook attachment
    (the dough can be made by hand but it's
    so much easier in a mixer)
large bowl or plastic container with a lid
sharp, serrated scoring knife or blade
    (I use my bread knife)
water spritzer bottle
baking parchment

## 1. Mixing

Place all the ingredients in the bowl of a stand mixer (or you can mix them by hand in a large bowl) and bring them together into a shaggy mess. This should take roughly 2 minutes. Tip the rough dough into a large, oiled bowl (or large, oiled plastic container with lid). Cover with cling film, if using a bowl (or put the lid on), and set aside for 30 minutes. It should be a wettish dough.

## 2. Stretching & Folding 1

After 30 minutes, liberally oil your hands. While the dough is still in the bowl, stretch and fold it over four times, turning the bowl by a quarter each time. The dough will feel quite stiff the first time you do this, but it will become easier as the gluten relaxes and the dough softens. Cover the bowl with cling film and set aside for another 30 minutes.

## 3. Stretching & Folding 2

Repeat step 2, above, two more times, stretching and folding the dough, leaving 30 minutes between each set. Each time, the dough will become softer and more pliable, and air bubbles should start to appear – try not to pop them. Repeat for a third time; at this point, I also push my fingers into the dough to create a dimpled effect, which seems to add more air. Cover and leave the dough to rest in the fridge overnight

(8 hours), if time allows – this will help to intensify the flavour of the loaf. If you are short of time, leave the dough for at least 1 hour, until risen and doubled in size.

### 4. Set the Oven
After a night in the fridge (or around 1 hour proving), take the dough out of the fridge. Preheat the oven to 240°C (220°C fan/475°F/Gas 9) – this is important, but if your oven doesn't reach such a high temperature, then set it to the highest it will go. It usually takes about 30 minutes to heat up, which is just enough time for shaping and a second prove.

### 5. Pre-Baking
To prepare the casserole dish (or ovenproof pot) for baking, cut a piece of baking parchment larger than the dish, then scrunch it into a ball. Open out the paper and lay it over the top of the dish, ready for the shaped dough.

### 6. Knock Back the Dough
Oil your work surface and hands, then gently tip the risen dough onto the oiled surface and knock back by gently pressing it into a rough, flattish, oval. (This process deflates the risen dough to remove any large air bubbles and evenly distributes the yeast. It also ensures an even-textured loaf when the dough is left to rise for a second time and finally baked.)

### 7. Shaping & Second Prove
Take a section of the dough, lift it (stretching it slightly), then fold it over towards the middle of the dough, pressing it down slightly. Continue working your way around the dough; it should start to form a smooth ball with large air bubbles trapped within. Flip the dough over so that the pinched middle is underneath. Using both hands in a cupped shape, work around the dough until it forms a ball; do this two or three times until it forms a perfect round shape. Lift it swiftly but

gently onto the baking parchment covering the dish, which should envelop it slightly as it sinks into the dish. Cover with the lid and set aside for 30 minutes for the second prove.

### 8. Spritzing, Flouring & Scoring
After 30 minutes, your dough will have risen by about half, and the oven should be at the correct temperature for baking. Spritz the top of the dough with water (or you can add a splash of water and wipe it over with your hand). Dust the top with flour and make a deep, wide slash across the dough using a sharp knife or blade. (I use my serrated bread knife).

### 9. Baking
Cover with the lid and place the dish in the preheated oven for 25 minutes. Carefully remove the lid and bake for another 20 minutes, until the bread is risen, golden, and crusty. Once baked, carefully remove the bread from the dish – it should sound hollow when tapped underneath if ready. Leave the loaf to cool completely (or for at least 1 hour) on a wire rack before slicing.

# Bru

# nch

Brunch must be the best meal of the day, or at least a close contender to Brinner (a combination of breakfast and dinner, and one that should be exclusively eaten in the evening). What I love about brunch is how it feels indulgent – the kind of food you could eat for breakfast, yet probably normally wouldn't. A brunch tends to last longer than either breakfast or even lunch, which lends a fabulous loucheness to the proceedings. It's about spending time with a partner and friends, rather than just eating for energy and leaving the table. There are also often cocktails involved, which adds another layer of indulgence and feasting.

# Upside Down Croque Madame

As kids, we would go on holiday to Mallorca with my cousins. Like typical young children, we'd expend a lot of energy and suddenly have an insatiable appetite. My mum, or auntie, would give us a small amount of money to go down to the fancy hotel in front of the apartment and order the only food they served at lunchtime: croque madame. It wasn't the best; simply melted cheese between two slices of white bread with ham and egg – but I loved those sandwiches. Here's my upside-down version comprising little squares of cheesy, hammy joy, draped in puff pastry, and baked until seriously golden and crisp, and then finished with a fried egg.

**Serves 2**

320g (11oz) sheet of ready-
   rolled puff pastry, roughly
   35 x 23cm (14 x 9in), or use
   homemade (see p12)
2 tsp Dijon mustard
drizzle of olive oil, plus extra
   for frying eggs
1 tsp thyme leaves
100g (3½oz) strong Cheddar,
   finely grated
2 shallots, cut into thin rings
6 thin slices of ham
4 square slices of Edam
1 egg, lightly beaten
2 eggs
salt and freshly ground
   black pepper

**YOU WILL NEED**
large baking tray, roughly
   38 x 27cm (15 x 10½in),
   lined with baking parchment

1 Preheat the oven to 220°C (200°C fan/425°F/Gas 7). Unroll the sheet of pastry and cut out two 14cm (5½in) squares. Spread 1 teaspoon of mustard over each square, leaving a narrow border around each one. Place in the fridge until needed.

2 Mark out 2 squares on the baking parchment, the same size as the pastry and with space between each one, and place drawn-side down on the baking tray. Drizzle generously with olive oil and sprinkle with thyme. Season with salt and pepper.

3 Scatter one-third of the grated cheese and a few rings of shallot over the marked squares. Ribbon 3 slices of ham on top of each one, followed by the rest of the grated cheese, divided evenly between the two, and the Edam slices.

4 Lay a square of puff pastry, mustard-side down, over each pile. Using the back of a teaspoon, scallop the edges of the pastry squares to seal. Score the top of each one in a diamond pattern with a sharp knife and then brush with egg.

5 Bake for 25 minutes, until the pastry is golden and crisp. Remove the tarts from the oven and allow them to sit on the tray for 5 minutes. While the tarts are resting, fry the eggs in a little olive oil in a frying pan to your liking.

6 Lay a piece of baking parchment on top of the tarts, followed by a chopping board, and carefully flip them over. Remove the tray and peel off the backing paper. Place the fried eggs on one of the squares and flip the second square on top (cheese-side down) to create a puff-pastry sandwich. Slice diagonally in half to serve.

# Coca de Verduras

This traditional Mallorquina "pizza" can be bought in any of the hundreds of *el forns* (bakeries), dotted around the island. While the literal translation of *coca de verduras* is "vegetable cake", it is more commonly known as Mallorcan pizza, and it's so delicious, unbelievably simple to make, and keeps well. I prefer to eat it at room temperature, which means it makes the ideal brunch or picnic dish.

**Serves 6**

**For the coca crust:**

375g (13oz) plain flour, plus extra for dusting
230ml (7¾fl oz) olive oil
230ml (7¾fl oz) sparkling water
1 tsp salt, plus extra for seasoning

**For the vegetable topping:**

1 handful of cherry tomatoes, chopped
½ red pepper, deseeded and diced
½ onion, diced
½ baby aubergine, diced
½ courgette, diced
1 garlic clove, grated
1 tbsp sweet smoked paprika
3 tbsp extra virgin olive oil
freshly ground black pepper

**YOU WILL NEED**

large baking tray, roughly 38 x 27cm (15 x 10½in), lined with baking parchment

1　Preheat the oven to 200°C (180°C fan/400°F/Gas 6). To make the coca crust, place half of the flour into a large bowl. Add the olive oil, sparkling water, and salt, then mix with your hands or a wooden spoon until the dough starts to come together. Add more flour, a little at a time, until the dough is no longer sticky; you may need to add a little more or less than the amount stated. Shape the dough into a smooth ball – it is ready to use straight away and there is no need to leave it to rest.

2　Turn the dough out onto the lined baking sheet/tray and gently press it out into a rough rectangular shape. It should be an even thickness all over, about the same as a regular pizza. Bake the crust for 15 minutes, or until the top starts to turn golden.

3　While the crust is baking, place all the chopped vegetables with the garlic, smoked paprika, and 1 tablespoon of olive oil into a large bowl. Season with salt and pepper and toss together.

4　Remove the crust from the oven when golden. Turn the oven up to 220°C (200°C fan/425°F/Gas 7). Spoon the vegetable mixture on top of the crust, leaving a narrow border around the edge. Pop the coca back into the oven for another 15–20 minutes, until the veg is tender and golden in places.

5　Drizzle the top with the remaining 2 tablespoons of extra virgin olive oil and a final generous sprinkling of salt. Traditionally, coca is served cut into squares.

# Leek, Sweetcorn & Tuna Fritters

I'm regularly asked about living with a vegetarian... how I cope with having to prepare two meals each day, and I often want to give my smart-aleck answer of "like every good housewife, I get up at 3am". Usually, I end up telling the truth, which is that I mostly eat vegetarian food myself. On occasion, I prepare what I call a "split dish", where I'll make the base of something that can either have a vegetarian or meat/fish protein added to it at the end. These fritters are a delicious example of this. The key ingredients are mixed in a bowl, then I separate half of it out and mix my half with a tin of tuna, and his half with a can of chickpeas. Sorted.

## Makes 6–8

30g (1oz) salted butter, plus extra for frying the fritters
1 tbsp olive oil, plus extra for frying the fritters
1 leek, chopped
4–5 Brussels sprouts, shredded
large handful of chopped herbs (leaves and stalks), such as dill and coriander
6 tbsp semolina flour (or plain flour)
2 heaped tbsp cottage cheese
2 large eggs
3 tbsp sweetcorn (frozen or canned), defrosted or drained as needed
200g (7oz) can tuna in olive oil, drained
400g (14oz) can chickpeas, drained
salt and freshly ground black pepper
salad leaves and lemon and lime wedges, to serve

1  Heat the butter and oil in a large sauté pan on a medium heat. Add the leek and sprouts and sauté, stirring occasionally, for 8 minutes, until tender. Set aside to cool slightly.

2  Tip the sautéed vegetables into a large bowl, add the herbs and season with plenty of salt and pepper. Stir in 2 heaped tablespoons of the flour, the cottage cheese, eggs, and the sweetcorn until combined.

3  Spoon half of the mixture into a second bowl. To one bowl, add the tuna and to the other, add two-thirds of the chickpeas (the remaining third can go into the bowl with the tuna, if you like).

4  Mash the chickpeas with the back of a fork and combine with the rest of the ingredients in the bowl – you may need to add another tablespoon of flour to each bowl to allow everything to come together.

5  Take one of the bowls and form the mixture into 3–4 patties with your hands. Repeat with the mixture in the second bowl.

6  Heat extra butter and oil in a large sauté or frying pan over a medium heat. Add the fritters and cook in two batches for 4 minutes on each side until set and golden. Place the cooked fritters in a warm oven until you're ready to serve. (Any leftovers will keep in the fridge for 3 days, or leave to cool and freeze for up to 3 months.)

7  Serve the fritters on a bed of salad leaves with lemon and lime wedges for squeezing over.

# Upside Down Tomato & Pesto Tarts

There's something about the combination of fresh sun-ripened tomatoes with basil pesto that reminds me of summers in the Med. We live off Caprese salads when in Mallorca, and I wanted to capture the fabulous combination of tomato, mozzarella, and basil but in an upside-down tart form.

**Serves 3**

320g (11oz) sheet of ready-rolled puff pastry, roughly 35 x 23cm (14 x 9in), or use homemade (see p12)
drizzle of olive oil
drizzle of balsamic vinegar
3 heirloom tomatoes, cut into thick slices (you can use a mix of colours, if liked)
1 egg, lightly beaten
salt and freshly ground black pepper

**For the cream cheese pesto:**
80g (2¾oz) pine nuts
30g (1oz) basil leaves
2 tbsp olive oil
75g (2½oz) good-quality cream cheese
1 garlic clove, peeled (optional)

**YOU WILL NEED**
large baking tray, roughly 38 x 27cm (15 x 10½in), lined with baking parchment

1   Preheat the oven to 220°C (200°C fan/425°F/Gas 7). Remove the pastry from the fridge and set aside.

2   Start to make the cream cheese pesto. Toast the pine nuts in a dry frying pan over a medium heat for roughly 5 minutes, shaking the pan regularly to prevent them from burning, until golden. Tip them into a bowl and set aside to cool.

3   Mark out 3 rectangles on the baking parchment, each roughly 11.5 x 7.5cm (4½ x 3in) and leaving space between each one, then place drawn-side down on the baking tray. Drizzle olive oil all over the lined baking tray, then add a sprinkling of balsamic vinegar, and season well with salt and pepper.

4   Arrange a third of the sliced tomatoes in a row on one of the marked rectangles, slightly overlapping the slices. Repeat with the remaining sliced tomatoes. Set aside.

5   To finish the pesto, add the pine nuts (reserving a few to garnish), basil, olive oil, cream cheese, and garlic, if using, to a blender. Season with salt and pepper and whizz to a fine paste.

6   Unroll the sheet of pastry and divide into three equal rectangles, the same size as those marked on the baking parchment. Slather the cream cheese pesto over the pastry rectangles, leaving a narrow border around each one.

7   Drape a pastry rectangle, pesto-side down, over each row of tomatoes. Using the back of a spoon, scallop the edges of the pastry to seal. Score the top of each puff in a diamond pattern with a sharp knife and then brush with egg.

8   Bake for 25–35 minutes, until the pastry is golden and crisp. Remove the tarts from the oven and allow them to sit on the tray for 5 minutes. Lay a piece of baking parchment on top, followed by a chopping board and deftly flip the tarts over. Remove the tray and peel off the backing paper. Scatter with the reserved pine nuts to serve.

# Asparagus, Pea & Potato Frittata

Before we bought our home in Mallorca, we used to stay in a little six-room hotel in Pollença Old Town. Every morning the whole building would be filled with the aroma of frittata slowly cooking on the stove top. They would put it out for breakfast, and any leftovers would be left for midday snacks. This frittata is perfect for a brunch as it can be made ahead, and is just as delicious eaten hot or cold. It can be adapted to suit the time of the year, too, by using different types of seasonal veg.

**Serves 6**

100ml (3½fl oz) extra virgin
  olive oil
400g (14oz) potatoes, such as
  Maris Piper, cut into small,
  even-sized chunks (no need
  to peel, if you prefer)
12 asparagus spears, tips left
  whole and stalks thinly sliced
handful of dill, fronds chopped
handful of thyme, leaves
  chopped
100g (3½oz) frozen peas
8 large eggs
salt and freshly ground
  black pepper
mixed leaf salad, to serve

**YOU WILL NEED**
25cm (10in) non-stick frying
  pan with lid

1   Heat the olive oil in the frying pan on a medium heat, and when it's nice and hot, turn down the heat to the lowest setting. Add the potatoes and cook gently, stirring occasionally, partially covered with the lid, for roughly 15 minutes, until softened and beginning to colour. Stir in the asparagus and herbs, then season with salt and pepper. Cover with the lid and allow the vegetables to sweat for another 5 minutes.

2   Carefully tip the potato and asparagus mixture into a colander to drain over a large bowl, then pour the oil back into the frying pan. Once drained, put the vegetables in the bowl and stir in the frozen peas.

3   Beat the eggs in a small bowl. Pour them over the vegetables, season with plenty of salt and pepper, and stir until combined. Leave to sit while you reheat the pan over a low heat.

4   Tip the egg mixture into the pan, spread out the vegetables so they evenly cover the base, and cook gently for about 5 minutes without doing anything. When the egg starts to set around the edge, use a spatula to shape the frittata into a cushion by gently drawing in the sides and gently tipping the pan to flood the empty space.

5   When the egg is almost set with a little liquid still visible on the top, take the pan off the heat and leave to stand for 4 minutes to cool a little. Place a large dinner plate on top of the pan and carefully flip the pan so that the frittata is now on the plate. Slide it back into the pan to cook the underneath for a few more minutes until it is set and lightly golden. (If you feel the frittata needs it, turn it twice more, cooking each side briefly and pressing the edges to retain the cushion shape.)

6   Leave the frittata to stand for 10 minutes before serving it cut into wedges. Serve with a mixed leaf salad.

# Cheesy Leek & Potato Galette

Looking for a quick meal that's easy to make and doesn't compromise on flavour? A galette is a great choice; it's essentially a rustic pastry pizza, and the choice of toppings is endless. I went for potatoes and leeks because that's what I had in the fridge, but you can get creative with whatever you have to hand. Cheese is involved, because what is life without cheese. I also used my homemade Cheese & Herb Shortcrust Pastry (see p13), but plain shop-bought would be just as good. The galette is perfect warm or made the day before and served at room temperature.

**Serves 4–6**

1 recipe quantity Cheese & Herb Shortcrust Pastry (see p13) or use 320g (11oz) sheet of ready-rolled shortcrust pastry

**For the filling:**
2 tbsp olive oil
30g (1oz) lightly salted butter
5–6 baby new potatoes, cut into 5mm (¼in) thick round slices
1 tsp chopped thyme leaves
2 leeks, thinly sliced
150g (5½oz) cream cheese
75g (2½oz) strong Cheddar, finely grated
flour, for dusting
1 egg, lightly beaten
1 tsp each of sesame seeds and poppy seeds, mixed (or extra grated cheese)
salt and freshly ground black pepper

**YOU WILL NEED**
large baking tray, roughly 38 x 27cm (15 x 10½in), lined with baking parchment

1   Make the pastry following the instructions on page 13 (it can be made in advance and will keep in the fridge for up to 24 hours or in the freezer for 3 months).

2   To make the filling, heat the olive oil and butter in a large frying pan (with a lid) on a medium heat. Add the potatoes and stir well to coat them in the buttery oil, then add the thyme, and season with salt and pepper. Sauté the potatoes for 5 minutes, turning them regularly. Turn the heat down to low, cover with the lid and allow the potatoes to sweat for a further 5 minutes, until just soft. Stir in the leeks and sauté gently, covered, for another 7 minutes, until tender.

3   Take the pan off the heat, let the potatoes and leeks cool for a minute or two, and then stir in the cream cheese and Cheddar. Set aside to cool completely.

4   Preheat the oven to 200°C (180°C fan/400°F/Gas 6). Dust your work surface with flour and roll out the pastry to a large, rough rectangle, about 3mm (⅛in) thick. It's fine if it has craggy edges and isn't perfect; this is the rustic look we're going for. Carefully transfer the pastry to the lined baking tray – it should slightly overhang the edges.

5   Tip the leek and potato filling into the centre of the pastry and spread it out evenly, leaving a 4cm (1½in) border. Carefully fold the edge of the pastry over the filling in sections, folding and overlapping it as you work around the galette. Brush the pastry with egg and sprinkle with seeds or more grated cheese.

6   Bake for 30 minutes, or until golden brown and crisp. Remove the galette from the oven and allow it to sit on the tray for 5 minutes before serving warm. Alternatively, leave to cool and store in the fridge to eat the next day. Bring back to room temperature before serving.

# Upside Down Eggs Benedict Tarts

Eggs Benedict is synonymous with brunch, and I wanted to create an all-in-one, upside-down tart version that replaces the muffin part with puff pastry. It's also easier to make as you can be cooking the trickiest part, the poached eggs, while the pie is in the oven.

## Serves 4

320g (11oz) sheet of ready-
  rolled puff pastry, roughly
  35 x 23cm (14 x 9in),
  or use homemade (see p12)
drizzle of olive oil
1 tsp chopped sage leaves
200g (7oz) baby leaf spinach,
  roughly chopped
200g (7oz) thinly sliced ham,
  roughly chopped
1 tsp chopped dill fronds
1 egg, lightly beaten
salt and freshly ground
  black pepper

### For the hollandaise sauce:
115g (4oz) unsalted butter,
  cut into pieces
3 large egg yolks
juice of ½ lemon
1 tsp Dijon mustard
pinch of cayenne pepper,
  plus extra to serve (optional)

### To serve:
4 eggs, at room temperature,
  for poaching
1 tbsp finely chopped chives

### YOU WILL NEED
large baking tray, roughly
  38 x 27cm (15 x 10½in),
  lined with baking parchment

1  Preheat the oven to 220°C (200°C fan/425°F/Gas 7). Unroll the sheet of pastry and cut it into quarters, each about 11 x 17cm (4½ x 6½in). Place in the fridge until needed.

2  Mark out 4 rectangles on the baking parchment, the same size as the pastry and with space between each one, and place drawn-side down on the baking tray. Drizzle generously with olive oil and sprinkle with sage. Season with salt and pepper.

3  Place the spinach and ham in a large bowl along with the dill and a drizzle of olive oil. Season with salt and pepper, and mix well. Leaving a 1cm (½in) border, spoon the ham and spinach mixture over the marked rectangles, then drape the pastry over the top. Using the back of a teaspoon, scallop the edges of the pastry to seal. Score the top of each tart in a diamond pattern with a sharp knife and then brush with egg. Bake the tarts for 25 minutes, until golden and crisp.

4  Meanwhile, make the hollandaise. Melt the butter in a small saucepan. Add the egg yolks, lemon juice, Dijon, cayenne pepper, and a pinch of salt to a blender and blend for 5 seconds, until combined. With the blender running on medium–high, slowly add the hot butter in a steady stream until the mix has emulsified into a smooth sauce. Set aside, covered, to keep warm.

5  Bring a large pan of water to the boil, ready to poach the eggs. When the tarts are ready, remove from the oven and allow them to sit while you poach the eggs. Crack one of the eggs into a ramekin. When the water in the pan comes to the boil, turn the heat down to medium–low and swirl the water with a spoon. Lower the egg into the water and repeat with three more eggs. Gently poach the eggs for 4 minutes for a medium-set yolk, then lift out with a slotted spoon onto a plate to drain.

6  Lay a piece of baking parchment on top of the tarts, followed by a chopping board and carefully flip them over. Remove the tray and peel off the backing paper. Place the poached eggs on top of the tarts and spoon over the sauce. Top with a sprinkling of cayenne or ground black pepper and the chopped chives.

# California Tortilla Bake with Spicy Potatoes

The Fig Tree is a wonderful beachside cafe in Venice, Los Angeles, that holds many wonderful memories for me and my husband, The Viking. The setting is glorious, with views of the Pacific Ocean and all the incredible people passing by. The food at the cafe is that typical LA mix of Californian and Mexican cuisines, and their breakfast potatoes are to die for. I have tried to recreate the essence of my favourite dish here as an easy brunch feast.

**Serves 6–8**

1 onion, roughly chopped
1 yellow and 1 red pepper,
    deseeded and sliced
2 large flat mushrooms,
    thickly sliced
drizzle of olive oil
2 tbsp chipotle fajita
    seasoning mix
200g (7oz) thinly sliced ham,
    chopped (optional)
2 slightly under-ripe avocados,
    peeled and cut into chunks
6 medium tortilla wraps
4 tbsp soured cream
100g (3½oz) strong cheese,
    grated (I use Cheddar)
salt and freshly ground
    black pepper

**For the spicy potatoes:**
4 large potatoes, cut into small
cubes (no need to peel)
30g (1oz) salted butter

**To serve:**
2 large handfuls of cherry
    tomatoes, cut in half
2 tbsp finely chopped chives
1 lime, cut into quarters

**YOU WILL NEED**
large ovenproof dish

1 Preheat the oven to 200°C (180°C fan/400°F/Gas 6).

2 Spread the onion, peppers, and mushrooms out in a large roasting tin, and drizzle with plenty of olive oil, then sprinkle with half of the chipotle seasoning mix, and plenty of salt and pepper. Mix everything together, coating the vegetables in the seasoned oil, cover the tin with foil and roast in the oven for 20 minutes. Remove the foil and cook for a further 15 minutes, or until the vegetables are soft and beginning to char a little at the edges. Stir in the ham, if using, and avocados. Leave to cool.

3 To assemble, take a tortilla wrap and spread a healthy spoonful of the soured cream over the top. Spoon one-sixth of the spicy vegetables down the middle and scatter over some of the cheese. Roll up the wrap tightly, then continue until you have made six rolled wraps. Cut the wraps into thirds and stand each one upright in the ovenproof dish. Sprinkle the top with more cheese and bake for 15 minutes, or until the cheese has melted, and the tortillas are heated through and golden.

4 Meanwhile, cook the potatoes in a pan of boiling salted water for 4 minutes, until just tender. Drain well, then return them to the pan and drizzle with olive oil and add the remaining chipotle mix. Toss the potatoes until coated in the seasoned oil.

5 Add a drizzle of olive oil and the butter to a frying pan with a lid and place on a medium heat. Add the potatoes and fry for 8 minutes, turning regularly. Cover with the lid and let the potatoes sweat for 5 minutes, then remove the lid, turn the heat up to high and cook for a final 5 minutes, until golden all over.

6 Serve the wraps with a little more soured cream, if liked, some fresh tomatoes, and chopped chives sprinkled on top. Finish with the potatoes and wedges of lime on the side.

# Vegetarian Full English Breakfast Terrine

The idea of a terrine is quite retro, but remember I'm a child of the '70s and '80s! It has all the elements of a classic full English breakfast, just delivered in slice form, and if you've never tried cream cheese mixed with baked beans, then quite frankly, you haven't lived! If you prefer, swap the veggie sausages for a meaty alternative.

**Serves 8–10**

drizzle of olive oil, plus extra
   for greasing
2 vegetarian sausages (or
   meaty alternative)
6 hash browns
600g (1lb 5oz) mushrooms,
   roughly chopped
1 tsp finely chopped rosemary
   leaves
4 large eggs
splash of whole milk
200g (7oz) can baked beans
400g (14oz) cream cheese
500g (1lb 2oz) spinach leaves
salt and freshly ground
   black pepper
slices of toast, to serve

**YOU WILL NEED**
large baking tray
small baking tray, about the
   same size as the loaf tin,
   lightly oiled
25 x 11cm (10 x 4½in) loaf tin,
   oiled, and lined with cling
   film, leaving an overhang

1   Preheat the oven to 200°C (180°C fan/400°F/Gas 6). Drizzle a little olive oil over a large baking tray and place the sausages, hash browns, and mushrooms on the tray. Scatter over the rosemary, then season with salt and pepper. Drizzle with a little more oil and cook in the oven for 25–35 minutes, until everything is beautifully golden. Set aside to cool.

2   Meanwhile, in a bowl, beat the eggs with a splash of milk. Season with salt and pepper, then pour the mixture into a small, oiled baking tray. Place in the oven, below the baking tray, and cook for 8 minutes, or until set. Set aside to cool.

3   In a large bowl, mix the baked beans with the cream cheese. Set aside.

4   Place a frying pan on a medium heat and add a drizzle of olive oil. Add the spinach, cover with a lid, and cook for 8 minutes, or until the leaves have wilted. Season with salt and pepper, and leave the spinach to cool.

5   Once everything is cooked and cooled, you're ready to build the terrine. Cut the sausages in half lengthways and lay them, cut-side up, in the bottom of the lined loaf tin. Next, add half of the bean and cream cheese mixture, spreading it out evenly. Spoon half of the spinach evenly on top.

6   Cut the baked omelette in half lengthways and lay one half on top of the spinach, followed by the remaining beany cream cheese, and a layer of hash browns. Spoon the remaining spinach over, followed by all the mushrooms. Top with a final layer of the baked omelette. Fold the overhanging cling film tightly over the top of the terrine and place two heavy weights on top. Place the terrine in the fridge and leave to set for at least 8 hours, preferably overnight.

7   To serve, peel back the top layer of cling film, lay a chopping board on top and flip it over. Carefully lift off the tin and gently peel back the cling film. Cut into thick slices and serve on toast.

# Baked "Shakshuka" Tarts

Baking eggs in this Middle Eastern-inspired spicy tomato sauce takes them to another level, while the crispy crunch of the filo pastry cases brings so much acoustic joy. Cooking the tarts in a muffin tray is a great way to serve multiple people the same dish with no fuss. You can also adapt the quantity you make, depending on the size of the gathering and your muffin tray. The spicy tomato sauce can be made ahead and kept in the fridge or freezer (see below).

## Makes 9

250g (9oz) pack of filo pastry
 (you need 9 sheets)
olive oil, for brushing
9 eggs (if using a 9-hole
 muffin tray)
100g (3½oz) feta, crumbled
chopped coriander, to serve

### For the spicy tomato sauce:
(makes roughly 300ml/10fl oz)

drizzle of extra-virgin olive oil
½ onion, finely chopped
2 garlic cloves, finely grated
1 red pepper, deseeded and
 finely chopped
1 tsp ground cumin
1 tsp paprika
1 tsp chilli flakes
2 x 400g (14oz) cans chopped
 tomatoes
300ml (10fl oz) vegetable stock
1 tsp tomato paste
1 tbsp red wine vinegar
pinch of sugar
salt and freshly ground
 black pepper

### YOU WILL NEED
9-hole muffin tin, brushed
 liberally with olive oil

1  Start with the spicy tomato sauce (it can be made up to 3 days in advance and kept in the fridge or frozen for 3 months; defrost thoroughly before use). Heat a little extra-virgin olive oil in a casserole pan on a medium heat. Add the onion and sauté, stirring often, for 6 minutes, until softened. Stir in the garlic, red pepper, and the spices and cook gently for a further 4 minutes, or until the onion starts to colour and the pepper is soft.

2  Pour in the canned tomatoes, then re-fill the cans with the stock, swish around to remove any tomatoey residue and add to the pan. Stir in the tomato paste, vinegar, and sugar, then season well with salt and pepper. Allow the sauce to come up to the boil, then turn the heat down to the lowest setting, and gently simmer for 1 hour, until thickened and reduced by half. Leave the sauce to cool.

3  Preheat the oven to 180°C (160°C fan/350°F/Gas 4). To make the filo cups, unroll the pastry sheets and cut one into quarters. Brush each quarter of filo liberally with olive oil and carefully press them into one of the muffin cups in the tray, overlapping the pastry slightly as you work around the cup until the base and sides are lined. Repeat to make 9 filo cups in total.

4  Once all the muffin cups are lined with filo, carefully spoon in the cooled, spicy tomato sauce, until roughly filled by half. Crack an egg into each muffin cup on top of the sauce.

5  Place the tray in the oven and bake for 20–25 minutes, or until the eggs are cooked to your liking, and the filo is golden and crisp. Remove from the oven and crumble over the feta. Season with salt and pepper and finish with a sprinkling of coriander.

# Upside Down French Toast

I absolutely love French toast, but frustratingly, The Viking isn't a fan of sweet things for breakfast or brunch, so we rarely have it. This upside-down version is a wonderfully sweet and jammy mess of a dish, and the great thing is that you can make it as big or as small as you like – a whole tray for a large gathering or a single slice as a mini feast just for you.

**Serves 4**

4 large eggs
100ml (3½fl oz) whole milk
1 tsp vanilla extract
½ tsp ground cinnamon
maple syrup, for drizzling
75g (2½oz) salted butter
100g (3½oz) chopped walnuts
100g (3½oz) strawberries,
    hulled and cut in half
100g (3½oz) blueberries
4 thick slices of brioche
75g (2½oz) demerara sugar
icing sugar, for dusting
    (optional)
whipped double cream or
    clotted cream, to serve

**YOU WILL NEED**
large baking tray, roughly
    38 x 27cm (15 x 10½in),
    lined with baking parchment

1   Preheat the oven to 200°C (180°C fan/400°F/Gas 6). Crack the eggs into a large bowl and whisk in the milk, vanilla, and cinnamon. Set aside.

2   Drizzle the lined baking tray with a generous amount of maple syrup, then dot small knobs of butter all over. Scatter over the walnuts and half of the strawberries and blueberries (dot them randomly over the tray).

3   Dip the slices of brioche into the egg mixture and place them on top of the berries and nuts. (I prefer to slightly overlap the slices in a random pattern to allow the corners and edges sticking up to become extra golden and crunchy.) Sprinkle the top with demerara sugar.

4   Bake for 20–25 minutes, until the top of the bread is golden. Remove the brioche from the oven and let it sit on the tray for 5 minutes. Lay a piece of baking parchment on top, followed by a chopping board and carefully flip it over. Remove the tray and peel off the backing paper.

5   Decorate the top of the brioche with the remaining berries, a good drizzle of maple syrup, and a dusting of icing sugar, if liked. Serve with whipped or clotted cream by the side.

# Mimosa Swirl Buns

I like to accompany a special brunch with a mimosa (or a buck's fizz as it's known here in the UK). This classic, tipsy orange juice cocktail is the perfect boujee way to start drinking early! These swirly buns capture all the flavour and sparkle of a classic mimosa but in glorious dough form.

## Makes 6

### For the buns:
200ml (7fl oz) whole milk
75g (2½oz) unsalted butter,
   plus extra for greasing
finely grated zest of 1 orange
100ml (3½fl oz) Champagne
500g (1lb 2oz) strong white
   bread flour, plus extra
   for dusting
30g (1oz) caster sugar
1 tsp salt
7g packet (2¼ tsp) instant
   dried yeast
1 large egg, lightly beaten

### For the filling:
100g (3½oz) soft light
   brown sugar
finely grated zest of 3 oranges
100g (3½oz) unsalted butter,
   softened and cut into cubes

### For the glaze:
150g (5½oz) cream cheese
2–3 tbsp icing sugar, sifted
splash of Champagne
finely grated zest of 1 orange

### YOU WILL NEED
30 x 20cm (12 x 8in) baking
   tin, greased, and base-lined
   with baking parchment

1 First, start the bun dough. Heat the milk, butter, and orange zest in a small saucepan over a medium-low heat until the butter melts. Leave to cool until just lukewarm, then pour in the Champagne – it may curdle a bit, but that is fine.

2 Mix the flour, caster sugar, salt, and yeast in a large bowl. Make a well in the middle, then pour in the lukewarm milk mixture and add the egg. Mix with your hands to form a rough, soft dough. Tip the dough out onto a lightly floured work surface and knead for 10–15 minutes, until smooth and elastic. (You can also do this in a stand mixer, using the dough hook on low speed for 10 minutes.) Place the dough in a lightly greased, clean bowl, cover with cling film and leave to rise in a warm place for 2 hours, or until doubled in size.

3 Meanwhile, make the filling. Place the brown sugar and orange zest in a bowl, then rub together using your fingertips to release the essential oils in the zest. Add the butter and mix well until combined to a paste. Set aside.

4 Once the dough has risen, tip it out onto a lightly floured work surface and use a rolling pin to roll it into a 40 x 50cm (15 x 19in) rectangle. Using a spoon or spatula, spread the orange butter in an even layer over the surface of the dough. Working from one of the long sides, roll up the dough into a cylinder, keeping the spiral tight. Using a sharp knife, cut the dough into 6 thick, even slices.

5 Arrange the buns, cut-side up, snugly in the base of the greased and lined baking tin. Cover the tin with cling film and leave the buns to prove for 45–60 minutes, until risen and puffy.

6 Preheat the oven to 180°C (160°C fan/350°F/Gas 4). Once proved, bake the buns for 30–40 minutes, or until risen and golden brown. While the buns are baking, prepare the glaze. Mix all the ingredients in a bowl until you have a runny icing.

7 Remove the buns from the oven and let them sit for 10 minutes in the tin on a wire rack. Drizzle or spread the icing over the top of each warm bun in a swirly pattern before serving.

# Picni

# Lun

cs &
ches

Growing up in 70s suburban London, our family picnics were not
made up of cucumber sandwiches served from a wicker basket while
sitting on a blanket on a grassy hillock. We did, however, have the
occasional huddle behind a windbreak on Scarborough Beach, with
some sandwiches served out of a Tupperware box. Mum preferred to
cater for a summer party at home, with guests choosing from a table
(indoors) laden with her version of picnic delights: classic finger foods,
robust pastry-filled items, sandwiches, and quiches galore. While
my family didn't necessarily embrace the outdoorsy picnic life, we
knew how to eat a good spread of picky bits, and that's what I'm
celebrating in this chapter.

# Three Dips in 90 Seconds

What's a picnic without a dip? These three dips are ridiculously simple to make, and hands down taste better than anything shop-bought. I'm serving them with my Poppy & Fennel Seed Crackers (see p51) and Cheat's Ciabatta Crostini (see p52), which are drenched in herby oil, before being toasted in the oven until crisp and golden.

**Serves about 10**

**YOU WILL NEED**
blender or food processor, baking sheet

### Cheese & Onion Dip

I use cottage cheese for this, which has a slight sharpness that works with the spring onion, chives, and Cheddar. Don't worry if you're not a fan of the texture of cottage cheese, blending turns it thick, creamy, and smooth.

**Ingredients**
300g (10oz) cottage cheese
1 bunch of fresh chives
½ spring onion
75g (2½oz) strong Cheddar, cut into small pieces
1 tbsp olive oil, plus extra to serve
salt and freshly ground black pepper

Place everything in a blender or food processor and whizz until smooth and creamy. Season with salt and pepper, to taste. Spoon into a bowl, drizzle with extra olive oil and top with a grinding of black pepper, to serve.

### My Tzatziki

You don't even need a blender to make this. Simply stir the ingredients together and tah dah – you have a creamy, herby, zesty dip.

**Ingredients**
300g (10oz) Greek yogurt
¼ cucumber, cut into very small dice
1 tbsp chopped dill
½ tbsp chopped mint leaves
finely grated zest of ½ lime
½ tsp garlic salt
1 tbsp olive oil

Place everything in a bowl (setting aside some of the cucumber and dill to serve) and mix well until combined. Spoon into a serving bowl and top with the reserved cucumber and dill.

### Olive & Chickpea Tapenade

Tapenade with a twist, thanks to the addition of garlic-stuffed green olives and chickpeas – all blended into a dip.

**Ingredients**
8 garlic-stuffed green olives
100g (3½oz) canned or jarred chickpeas, drained
large handful of coriander
2 tbsp olive oil, plus extra for drizzling
salt and freshly ground black pepper

Place everything in a food processor and pulse until roughly combined to a thick paste. Season with salt and pepper, to taste. Spoon into a serving bowl and drizzle with a little extra olive oil.

# Poppy & Fennel Seed Crackers

I'd never thought of making crackers before, which is utterly insane as we get through a huge amount of cheese in this household, and a cracker is the ultimate vehicle to get said cheese into one's gob. These little beauties are easy to make, and you can be quite inventive with the flavourings – just remember to keep it simple and elegant.

## Makes about 20

250g (9oz) plain flour, plus extra for rolling
50g (1¾oz) wholemeal or rye flour
2 tsp baking powder
85g (3oz) salted butter, softened and cut into small pieces
2 tsp fennel seeds
2 tsp poppy seeds
½ tsp flaky sea salt

### YOU WILL NEED
large baking sheet, lined with baking parchment
fluted cutting wheel or cookie cutters of your choice

1 Preheat the oven to 180°C (160°C fan/350°F/Gas 4).

2 Place both types of flour, the baking powder, butter, fennel and poppy seeds, and salt in a food processor and blitz to a crumbly mixture. Add 100ml (3½fl oz) water and pulse again until the mixture comes together into a dough.

3 Roll the dough out on a lightly floured work surface until about 5mm (¼in) thick. Cut the dough into your choice of shapes and sizes; I use a fluted cutting wheel to do this, adding to their homemade appeal, but you could use a round fluted cookie cutter, if preferred. Space the crackers out on the lined baking sheet and prick the tops all over with a fork.

4 Bake for 15–20 minutes, until the crackers start to crisp and turn golden around the edges; they may still be slightly soft but will firm up further when cold. Leave to cool on the baking sheet.

5 Serve with dips (see p48), chopped liver (p109), or the cheese of your choice. The crackers will keep in an airtight container for up to 1 week.

### Cook's Tip:
Try experimenting with different flavour combinations, including:
Rosemary and garlic salt
Thyme and lemon zest
Oregano & chilli (both dried)

# Cheat's Ciabatta Crostini

Need something to dunk into my dips (see p48) but don't have time to make crostini from scratch? This cheat's version still gives a homemade feel but in next to no time. I've made these with gluten-free ciabatta and regular ciabatta, and both work well.

## Makes about 20

100ml (3½fl oz) extra virgin
   olive oil or cold-pressed
   rapeseed oil
1 tbsp finely chopped rosemary
   leaves
1 tbsp finely chopped thyme
   leaves
½ tsp garlic salt
2 ciabatta loaves, thinly sliced
salt and freshly ground
   black pepper

### YOU WILL NEED
1–2 large baking sheets

1   Preheat the oven to 190°C (170°C fan/375°F/Gas 5).

2   Mix the olive oil with the herbs and garlic salt in a large bowl. Season with salt and pepper, then add the slices of ciabatta. Mix well to coat the ciabatta in the herby, garlicky oil.

3   Arrange the ciabatta slices over the baking sheet(s) and bake for 10–15 minutes, turning halfway, until toasted and golden. Leave to cool on the baking sheet. Transfer the crostini to an airtight container and store for up to 2 days.

# Grandma Sylvia's Cucumber Salad

My grandma, Sylvia, was a remarkable woman. A doctor's wife, she was fiercely intelligent and independent for a woman born at the turn of the last century. Her meals were hearty, homely, and delicious, and her cucumber salad was legendary! This is a traditional Jewish salad often served with salmon. It has Polish and Russian roots and would have originally used acetic acid, which you had to buy from the chemist. It's quite hard to find these days, so I've adapted it to the more widely available white wine vinegar.

**Serves 6–8**

1 whole cucumber
60g (2oz) caster sugar
120ml (4¼fl oz) warm water
2 tsp white wine vinegar
pinch of salt

**YOU WILL NEED**
mandoline or food processor

1 Slice the cucumber very finely into rounds or strips – a mandoline will make light work of this, but a food processor is safer! Place the cucumber in a large serving bowl.

2 In a small bowl, add the sugar and warm water, stir until dissolved, then leave the water to cool. Stir in the vinegar and salt, then pour the mixture over the sliced cucumber. Let the salad sit for at least 30 minutes before serving. It will stay fresh in the fridge for up to 4 days stored in an airtight container.

# My Potato Salad

There's a trend for fancy potato salads, from roasted and smashed to fully mashed, but what I haven't seen is a classic, creamy mayonnaise potato salad – the kind Mum used to make when we were kids. Here, the potatoes are boiled until soft, but not falling apart, and the mayonnaise is more like a dressing than a condiment, loosened with a splash of vinegar and water so it's not too thick or gloopy. Delicious.

## Serves 6

750g (1lb 10oz) baby new
   potatoes, cut in half
5 spring onions, thinly sliced
handful of mint leaves, finely
   chopped (optional)

### For the mayonnaise dressing:

2 egg yolks
1 heaped tsp Dijon mustard
½ tsp salt
1 tsp caster sugar
140ml (4½fl oz) cold-pressed
   rapeseed oil
3 tsp white wine vinegar
2 tsp lemon juice

### YOU WILL NEED
hand-held blender

1   Cook the potatoes in a large saucepan of salted boiling water until tender but not too soft. Drain the potatoes thoroughly and transfer them to a large serving bowl.

2   Meanwhile, make the mayonnaise dressing. Using a hand-held blender, blend all the ingredients with 1 tablespoon water until smooth. It should emulsify into a creamy, yet loose, dressing.

3   Pour the dressing into the bowl of potatoes, add the spring onions, and mix well until combined. Garnish with mint, if using, and serve while still warm, if possible.

# Upside Down Caprese Salad in a Jar

I adore this all-in-one salad in a jar; it makes picnics so easy, and there's also a little hint of drama as you turn the jar upside down to release the contents into a serving bowl. Good-quality, vine-ripened tomatoes are essential, and a classic vinaigrette is a must.

**Serves 2**

4 tbsp extra virgin olive oil
1 tsp Dijon mustard
1 tsp dried oregano
2 tbsp apple cider vinegar
2 large heritage tomatoes, thickly sliced
100g (3½oz) cherry tomatoes, quartered (I like to use orange or yellow ones)
1 large bunch of basil leaves
2 x 125g (4½oz) balls of mozzarella, drained and thickly sliced
1 large red onion, thinly sliced into rings
salt and freshly ground black pepper

**YOU WILL NEED**
1 litre (1¾ pint) large jar with lid

1   Add the olive oil, mustard, oregano, and vinegar to a jug, then mix together with a fork to make a dressing. Season with salt and pepper.

2   Arrange a layer of tomato (both sliced and quartered) in a 1 litre (1¾ pint) jar, followed by some basil leaves, and a layer of mozzarella. Add a layer of onion rings, then drizzle over some of the dressing. Repeat this layering until the jar is full, occasionally adding more of the dressing.

3   Put the lid on the jar and store the salad in the fridge. It will keep for up to 8–12 hours, but it is good to eat immediately. When ready to serve, open the jar and flip it over to tip the salad into a bowl.

# Roasted Beetroot, Feta & Green Bean Salad

Don't get me wrong, a sandwich has its place as part of a picnic, but I think a glorious salad can also be given room to shine. Both the beetroot and green beans in this salad can be prepared in advance and then put into a container for transporting. Assemble the salad once you're ready to eat.

**Serves 6**

**For the roasted beetroot:**
5 small raw beetroots, cut
   into wedges
½ red onion, cut into wedges
2 tbsp balsamic vinegar
2 tbsp cold-pressed
   rapeseed oil
1 tsp Dijon mustard
salt and freshly ground
   black pepper

**For the green beans:**
200g (7oz) fine green beans
1 tbsp cold-pressed
   rapeseed oil
finely grated zest and juice
   of 1 unwaxed lemon

**To serve**
80g (2¾oz) bag of rocket,
   watercress, and
   spinach salad
150g (5½oz) feta, crumbled
sesame seeds, for sprinkling

**YOU WILL NEED**
roasting tin

1   Preheat the oven to 190°C (170°C fan/375°F/Gas 5).

2   First prepare the roasted beetroot. Place the beetroot in a roasting tin with the rest of the ingredients and mix well. Season with salt and pepper. Roast the beetroot for roughly 45 minutes, turning regularly, until it is tender. Set aside to cool for 20 minutes.

3   Meanwhile, boil or steam the green beans until tender, roughly 4 minutes. Drain the beans well, if needed, and tip them into a bowl. While still warm, add the oil, and the zest and juice of the lemon. Stir well and set aside to cool.

4   To build your salad, add a base layer of salad leaves to a dish, top with the dressed green beans and then the roasted beetroot. Finish the salad with the crumbled feta and a sprinkling of sesame seeds. Season with salt and pepper before serving.

# The Best Ever Sausage Rolls

Sausage rolls always make an appearance when I'm making food for a picnic – and these ones are special, or so I'm told by friends who've tried them. They can be made meaty or vegetarian; simply swap out the pork sausages for your favourite vegetarian alternative. I recommend you go all out and make the "Ruff" Puff Pastry (see p12), although an all-butter, shop-bought alternative would also work well.

## Makes about 24

1 recipe quantity of "Ruff"
Puff Pastry (see p12) or
320g (11oz) sheet of
ready-rolled puff pastry,
roughly 35 x 23cm (14 x 9in)
85g (3oz) packet of sage and
onion stuffing mix
drizzle of olive oil
75g (2½oz) salted butter
1 large onion, finely chopped
200g (7oz) chestnut
mushrooms, finely chopped
1 tbsp chopped herbs, such as
rosemary and thyme
2 large garlic cloves, crushed
6 pork (or vegetarian) sausages
100g (3½oz) mature Cheddar,
grated
1 tsp English mustard
1 egg, lightly beaten
salt and freshly ground
black pepper

**YOU WILL NEED**
large baking tray, roughly
38 x 27cm (15 x 10½in),
lined with baking parchment

1   Preheat the oven to 180°C (160°C fan/350°F/Gas 4). Make the pastry following the instructions on page 12 or use ready-made. Place in the fridge until needed.

2   Make the stuffing mix in a large bowl according to the packet instructions, adding a drizzle of olive oil. Set aside.

3   Heat a drizzle of olive oil and the butter in a large frying pan on a medium heat. Add the onion and cook, stirring occasionally, for 5 minutes, then add the mushrooms and cook for a further 4 minutes. Stir in the herbs and garlic. Season with salt and pepper and cook for a final 5 minutes, until everything has softened and any liquid from the mushrooms has evaporated. Set aside.

4   Squeeze the sausages out of their skins into a large bowl and mash the sausagemeat with the back of a fork. Add the stuffing, the mushroom mixture, and Cheddar, and mix well. Set aside to cool.

5   Roll out 2 long strips of pastry, roughly 30 x 8cm (12 x 3¼in). (Save any leftover pastry for another recipe.) Spread the mustard over one side of each strip.

6   Split the sausage mixture in half and shape each half into a long log shape down the middle of each pastry strip. Wet the edges of the pastry with a little water before rolling them up, ensuring that the sealed edge is running along the bottom. Cut each roll into bite-sized slices, each about 3cm (1¼in). Brush the tops with egg and score each roll three times.

7   Place the sausage rolls on the lined baking tray and bake for 30 minutes, until golden and risen. Turn off the heat and leave the sausage rolls in the oven for 10 minutes to cool slightly before serving.

# Upside Down Scotch Egg Tart

The brilliant thing about a Scotch egg, much like a Cornish pasty, is that it's almost a meal in itself. For those not in the know, it's a hard-boiled egg, wrapped in sausagemeat, coated in breadcrumbs, and then deep-fried until golden and crisp. It's a classic British picnic item, and this is my upside-down tart version. It's delicious served with chutney or my Red Onion Jam (see p15).

## Serves 6

6 large eggs, at room
    temperature
320g (11oz) sheet of ready-
    rolled puff pastry, roughly
    35 x 23cm (14 x 9in), or use
    homemade (see p12)
6 tbsp olive oil
1 tsp chopped rosemary
125g (4½oz) fresh breadcrumbs
400g (14oz) sausagemeat (the
    inside of 6 sausages)
1 egg, lightly beaten
salt and freshly ground
    black pepper

### YOU WILL NEED
large baking tray, roughly
    38 x 27cm (15 x 10½in),
    lined with baking parchment
7.5cm (3in) round cutter

1  Bring a small saucepan of water to the boil on a high heat. Using a spoon, gently lower the eggs into the pan, reduce the heat by half and gently boil for 5 minutes. Immediately remove the eggs from the pan into a bowl of iced water. Allow them to cool for at least 10 minutes, then peel and set aside.

2  Preheat the oven to 180°C (160°C fan/350°F/Gas 4). Unroll the sheet of pastry and set aside.

3  Mark out a large rectangle on the baking parchment, the same size as the pastry. Using the cutter as a template, draw 6 discs evenly spaced apart on the paper. Place the paper drawn-side down on the baking tray. Drizzle generously with half of the olive oil and sprinkle with rosemary. Season with salt and pepper.

4  Spoon the breadcrumbs over the marked circles in a pile (roughly 20g/¾oz per circle). Drizzle the remaining oil over the breadcrumbs.

5  Divide the sausagemeat into 6 portions. Wrap a portion of sausagemeat around each of the hard-boiled eggs until enclosed in an even layer. Place an egg on top of each breadcrumb pile.

6  Drape the pastry sheet over the top to cover and press the pastry down between each sausagemeat-covered egg. Using the back of a spoon, scallop the edge of the pastry sheet to seal. Score the top in a diamond pattern with a sharp knife and then brush with egg.

7  Bake for 30 minutes, until the pastry is golden and crisp. Remove the tart from the oven and allow it to sit on the tray for 10 minutes. Lay a piece of baking parchment on top, followed by a chopping board, and carefully flip the tart over in one swift move. Remove the tray and peel off the backing paper. Cut into 6 squares to serve.

# Upside Down Smoked Salmon & Spinach Mini Quiches

No picnic or summer spread is complete without quiche. Mum has always been exceptional at preparing quiches, and they always make an appearance at gatherings. She makes multiple versions, then has them ready to go in the freezer. My upside-down version is so simple to make, and can also be frozen, ready for picnics to come.

**Makes 6**

320g (11oz) sheet of ready-rolled puff pastry, roughly 35 x 23cm (14 x 9in), or use homemade (see p12)
2 eggs, lightly beaten, plus 1 extra for glazing
1 tbsp cream cheese
2 tbsp Greek yogurt
1 large handful of fresh dill, chopped
100g (3½oz) smoked salmon, chopped
75g (2½oz) spinach leaves, finely chopped
drizzle of olive oil
1 tsp fresh thyme leaves
finely grated zest of 1 unwaxed lemon
salt and freshly ground black pepper

**YOU WILL NEED**
large baking tray, roughly 38 x 27cm (15 x 10½in), lined with baking parchment
10cm (4in) cookie cutter

1   Preheat the oven to 220°C (200°C fan/425°F/Gas 7). Unroll the sheet of pastry and, using the cookie cutter, stamp out 6 rounds. Place them on a tray in the fridge until needed.

2   Using the same cookie cutter as a template, draw 6 rounds onto the sheet of baking parchment, evenly spaced apart. Place the paper drawn-side down on the baking tray.

3   In a large bowl, beat 2 eggs, then add the cream cheese and yogurt. Season with salt and pepper, and stir in the dill to combine. Mix in the smoked salmon and spinach. Set aside.

4   Drizzle olive oil over the lined baking tray and sprinkle with thyme and lemon zest. Season with salt and pepper. Divide the quiche filling between the marked rounds, leaving a narrow border – don't worry if any liquid seeps out.

5   Drape the pastry discs over the quiche filling. Using the back of a teaspoon, scallop the edges of the pastry to seal. Score a cross in the top of each quiche with a sharp knife and then brush with egg.

6   Bake for 25–35 minutes, until the pastry is golden and crisp. Remove the quiches from the oven and allow them to sit on the tray for 5 minutes. Slide a spatula underneath each one and deftly flip them over to serve.

# Ploughman's Lunch Picnic Loaf

I'm definitely a picnic person over a barbecue one; I've always found barbecues to be a bit of a faff. I'd rather cook everything indoors and then transport it to a freshly mown lawn or to the beach to eat. And that's where this fabulous picnic loaf comes in. I've gone for the classic British flavours of a ploughman's, layered inside a large loaf. The joy of this is that it can – and should – be made the day before, to allow the flavours time to meld together. Pure picnic joy!

## Makes 1 large, filled loaf

1 large, round, crusty loaf (or My No-Knead "Sourdough" Bread on pages 16–17)
1 tbsp English mustard
2 tbsp mayonnaise
1 small Little Gem lettuce, leaves separated
6 slices of ham (I love a thick cut)
2 tbsp horseradish sauce
½ small cucumber, thinly sliced
150g (5½oz) strong Cheddar, thinly sliced
2 tbsp sandwich pickle (Branston is the obvious choice)
1 Scotch egg
100g (3½oz) coleslaw
4 mini pork pies
handful of pickles, such as baby pickled onions and cornichons
sea salt and freshly ground black pepper

1   Cut the top off your loaf to make a lid and scoop out most of the inside to leave room for the filling. (You can make breadcrumbs with the spare bread. It also freezes well.) Spread the inside of the loaf with half of the mustard and then half of the mayo.

2   Now, it's time to add the filling in layers. As with any good sandwich, it's important to consider structural integrity, so avoid layering slippery, moist things together. Remember to press down each layer as you go so that it's nice and firm, and to season with salt and pepper every few layers.

3   Add the layers in the following order (or you choose): lettuce leaves, ham, horseradish sauce, slices of cucumber, a third of the cheese, sandwich pickle, a whole Scotch egg, another third of the cheese, coleslaw, whole pork pies, a handful of pickles to fill in the gaps, and the remaining cheese. Spread the rest of the mustard and mayonnaise over the bread "lid" and place it on top of the loaf. Wrap the whole thing tightly in cling film and pop it in the fridge until ready to serve.

4   When ready to serve, cut the picnic loaf into slices or wedges. And devour!

# Quiche Susanna

This quiche is named after our wonderful food stylist, Susanna, who has beautifully cooked the food and styled the photographs for this and my previous book. Along with the crispy lardons of the classic quiche Lorraine, this version is made with beetroot pastry and also features one of Sus' favourite vegetables, fennel. Sweet with a hint of aniseed, fennel is the perfect accompaniment to the salty bacon, making it my new favourite flavour combination.

**Serves 8**

**For the beetroot pastry:**
150g (5½oz) cold salted butter, cut into cubes, plus extra for greasing
70g (2¼oz) cooked beetroot (not in vinegar), patted dry and grated
150g (5½oz) plain flour
100g (3½oz) rye flour
1 tsp each of finely chopped thyme and rosemary leaves
pinch of salt

**For the filling:**
drizzle of olive oil
150g (5½oz) lardons (or bacon, chopped into cubes)
1 fennel bulb, cut into thin wedges (don't trim)
1 tsp each of finely chopped thyme and rosemary leaves
4 eggs, lightly beaten
220g (scant 8oz) Greek yogurt
100ml (3½fl oz) single cream
salt and freshly ground black pepper
dill sprigs, to garnish

**YOU WILL NEED**
medium roasting tin
20cm (8in) fluted, loose-bottomed flan tin, greased

1 Make the pastry. Place the butter, beetroot, both types of flour, the herbs, and a pinch of salt in a food processor and whizz to a crumbly consistency (it may clump slightly, which is fine). Add a splash of cold water and blitz again until the pastry comes together into a smooth ball of dough – you may need to add a little more water. Wrap the pastry in cling film and chill for at least 30 minutes.

2 While the pastry is chilling, place a frying pan on a medium heat and add a drizzle of olive oil. Add the lardons or bacon and sauté, stirring regularly, for 8 minutes, or until golden and crisp. Lift out with a slotted spoon to drain on a plate, lined with kitchen paper, and set aside to cool.

3 Preheat the oven to 190°C (170°C fan/375°F/Gas 5). Place the fennel wedges in a roasting tin and sprinkle with the herbs. Season with a little salt and pepper and drizzle with olive oil. Stir well to coat the fennel in the seasoned oil and roast in the oven for 30 minutes, until tender but not too soft. Set aside.

4 Turn the oven down to 180°C (160°C fan/350°F/Gas 4). Remove the pastry from the fridge and roll it out on a lightly floured work surface into a round large enough to line the base and sides of the flan tin, and about 3mm (⅛in) thick. Trim the edge of the pastry, prick the base with a fork, and line with a piece of baking parchment. Fill the lined pastry case with baking beans and blind bake for 15 minutes, or until slightly golden around the edges. Lift out the paper and beans, then return the pastry case to the oven for another 10 minutes, or until cooked.

5 Beat the eggs, yogurt, and cream in a bowl. Season with salt and pepper, and stir in the cooled crispy lardons or bacon.

6 Arrange the fennel in the pastry case, then pour in the egg and cream mixture. Bake for 45 minutes, until golden and risen. Set aside on a wire rack to cool slightly. Remove the quiche from the tin, sprinkle with dill, and serve it cut into slices.

# Upside Down Summer Berry Sandwich

Every picnic or lunch needs something sweet, and this incredible dessert takes the classic strawberries and cream to a new level. Berries tend to turn mushy in the oven, but this is no bad thing here. When roasted, they turn into a perfect, sticky, jammy filling for a creamy, summery, puff pastry indulgence.

## Serves 2

320g (11oz) sheet of ready-rolled puff pastry, roughly 35 x 23cm (14 x 9in), or use homemade (see p12)
2 tbsp lemon and lime marmalade
3 tbsp runny honey
1 tbsp balsamic glaze
150g (5½oz) raspberries
100g (3½oz) blueberries
finely grated zest of 1 orange
1 egg, lightly beaten

### For the topping:
300ml (10fl oz) double cream
2 tbsp Greek yogurt
1 tbsp cream cheese
1 tbsp icing sugar, plus extra for dusting
100g (3½oz) strawberries, hulled and cut in half

### YOU WILL NEED
large baking tray, roughly 38 x 27cm (15 x 10½in), lined with baking parchment

1 Preheat the oven to 220°C (200°C fan/425°F/Gas 7). Unroll the sheet of pastry and cut out two 14cm (5½in) squares. Spread 1 tablespoon of the lemon and lime marmalade over each square, leaving a narrow border around the edge. Place in the fridge until needed.

2 Mark out 2 squares on the baking parchment, the same size as the pastry and with space between each one, and place drawn-side down on the baking tray. Drizzle the honey and balsamic glaze over. Divide the raspberries and blueberries between the 2 squares, piling them up in the centre. Sprinkle with the orange zest.

3 Lay a square of pastry, marmalade-side down, over each pile of berries. Using the back of a teaspoon, scallop the edge of the pastry squares to seal. Score the top in a diamond pattern with a sharp knife and then brush with egg.

4 Bake for 25 minutes, until the pastry is golden and crisp. Remove the tarts from the oven and allow them to sit on the tray for 5 minutes. Lay a piece of baking parchment on top, followed by a chopping board, and carefully flip the tarts over in one swift move. Remove the tray and peel off the backing paper. Leave to cool.

5 Meanwhile, finish the topping. Pour the double cream into a bowl and whisk to soft peaks with an electric hand whisk. Stir in the yogurt, cream cheese, and sugar and whisk again until firm but still soft and whippy.

6 Spoon the whipped cream over the two tarts, dividing it equally. Arrange the strawberries, cut-side down, on one of the tarts. Then place the second tart on top of the strawberries, cream-side down. Dust the top with icing sugar and cut diagonally in half to serve.

# Ever,
# Feas

# yday
# ting

Clearly, life isn't one endless round of parties, picnics, and brunches, but this doesn't mean that we can't add a little pizzazz to the everyday. Whether it's a family meal or movie night for one, the plan is to make each day feel a little special. Here's a collection of my favourite comfort meals, some given an upside-down twist and others pure classics. A few are slightly more time-consuming to make and perfect for weekends, while others take less time to prepare and are suitable for weekdays – all are easy, shareable, and generous. Perfect for everyday feasting.

# Upside Down Carrot & Coriander Tart

People sometimes ask, "Is there anything you can't turn upside down?" My answer is perhaps obvious – soup! Yet, I can still capture the flavours of my favourite soups in a tart. Carrot and coriander is a classic combination that works wonderfully cooked this way.

**Serves 4**

320g (11oz) sheet of ready-
 rolled puff pastry, roughly
 35 x 23cm (14 x 9in), or use
 homemade (see p12)
drizzle of olive oil
drizzle of runny honey
1 tsp thyme leaves, plus extra
 to serve
6 carrots, halved lengthways
1 egg, lightly beaten
salt and freshly ground
 black pepper

**For the coriander pesto:**
1 large handful of coriander
 leaves and stalks
50g (1¾oz) walnuts
1 garlic clove
80g (2¾oz) strong Cheddar,
 coarsely grated
2 tbsp olive oil

**YOU WILL NEED**
large baking tray, roughly
 38 x 27cm (15 x 10½in),
 lined with baking parchment

1   Preheat the oven to 220°C (200°C fan/425°F/Gas 7). Unroll the sheet of pastry and set aside.

2   Mark out a large rectangle on the baking parchment, the same size as the pastry, and place it drawn-side down on the baking tray. Drizzle olive oil and honey over the lined baking tray, then sprinkle with the thyme. Season with salt and pepper.

3   Leaving a 2cm (¾in) border, arrange the carrots cut-side down in 2 tight rows on the marked rectangle – each row of carrots should be placed lengthways on the baking parchment with the pointed ends facing towards the middle.

4   Place all the ingredients for the coriander pesto in a food processor and blitz to a coarse paste. Leaving a 1cm (½in) border, spread the pesto over one side of the pastry.

5   Drape the pastry, pesto-side down, over the carrots. Using the back of a teaspoon, scallop the edges of the pastry to seal. Score the top in a diamond pattern with a sharp knife and then brush with egg.

6   Bake for 30 minutes, until the pastry is golden and crisp. Remove the tart from the oven and allow it to sit on the tray for 5 minutes. Lay a piece of baking parchment on top, followed by a chopping board, and carefully flip it over. Remove the tray and peel off the backing paper. Cut into quarters and serve sprinkled with extra thyme, if you like.

# Upside Down Chicken Naan

Growing up, my local high street was home to many amazing Indian restaurants. The dishes I ate were often "tame" versions of traditional ones, as the originals were said to be too spicy or unusual for our unaccustomed palates. A lot has changed since, but I still adore a classic takeaway curry, and this one is inspired by a recipe from my friend, chef and "fakeaway" expert, Dean Edwards.

## Serves 4

25g (scant 1oz) ghee or
   vegetable oil
3 onions, sliced
2 carrots, diced
1 small red pepper, diced
2 tsp garlic paste
2 tsp ginger paste
2 tsp garam masala
¾ tsp ground turmeric
½ tsp paprika
200g (7oz) can plum tomatoes
2 tsp tomato paste

### For the naan dough:
120ml (4fl oz) warm water
7g packet (2¼ tsp) instant
   dried yeast
2 tsp golden caster sugar
300g (10oz) strong white bread
   flour, plus extra for dusting
½ tsp salt, plus extra to season
½ tsp baking powder
75g (2½oz) butter/ghee, melted
150ml (5fl oz) plain yogurt
1 tbsp nigella seeds

### For the topping:
1 onion, sliced
2 skinless, boneless chicken
   breasts, cut into chunks
freshly ground black pepper
1 handful of chopped coriander

### YOU WILL NEED
large baking tray, roughly
   38 x 27cm (15 x 10½in),
   lined with baking parchment

1   To make the curry sauce, heat the ghee or vegetable oil in a large pan over a medium–low heat. Add the onions, carrots, red pepper, garlic, and ginger and cook, stirring occasionally, for 20 minutes, until softened. Stir in the spices, canned tomatoes, and tomato paste, then pour in enough water to just cover the vegetables, about 250ml (9fl oz). Cover with the lid and simmer for 30 minutes. Leave to cool, then blend until smooth.

2   Meanwhile, make the naan dough. Pour the warm water into a bowl and sprinkle over the yeast and half of the sugar. Leave for 10–15 minutes, until frothy. In a large bowl, mix together the flour, remaining sugar, the salt, and baking powder. Make a well in the centre and pour in 30g (1oz) of the melted butter or ghee, the yogurt, nigella seeds, and yeast mixture. Using your hands, bring the mixture together. Knead the dough in the bowl until it comes together into a ball, then tip it out onto a well-floured surface and knead for another 10 minutes, or until smooth and elastic. Put the dough in a greased bowl, cover, and leave to rise in a warm place for about 1 hour, or until doubled in size.

3   Preheat the oven to 220°C (200°C fan/425°F/Gas 7). Leaving a 2cm (¾in) border, brush half of the remaining melted butter or ghee over the lined baking tray and season with salt and pepper. Scatter over half of the sliced onion and one of the chicken breasts, then spoon half of the cooled curry sauce on top. Repeat with the rest of the onion, the second chicken breast, and the remaining sauce.

4   Tip the naan dough out onto a lightly floured surface and gently roll it out to a rectangle, about 40 x 28cm (16 x 11in). Carefully lay the naan over the top of the curry and tuck in the edges. Brush the top with the remaining melted butter or ghee.

5   Bake for 25 minutes, or until the naan is risen and golden. Remove the chicken curry naan from the oven and leave it to sit on the tray for 10 minutes. Place a piece of baking parchment on top, followed by a chopping board and then carefully flip it over. Remove the tray and peel off the backing paper. Sprinkle with chopped coriander, to serve.

# Upside Down Smashed Burger Tarts

There has been a big trend for smashed burgers in recent years and I can totally understand why – they're so simple and the "smashing" of the meat patty to flatten it out ensures a quick and even cook. My twist uses ready-made meatballs and, of course, puff pastry, which turns these into little pies. They are wonderful served warm from the oven, topped with pickles and your favourite sauces.

**Makes 6**

320g (11oz) sheet of ready-
    rolled puff pastry, roughly
    35 x 23cm (14 x 9in), or use
    homemade (see p12)
6 tbsp Red Onion Jam (see
    p15), or use shop-bought
drizzle of olive oil
2 tsp thyme leaves
1 red onion, thinly sliced
    into rings
6 beef meatballs (I use
    ready-made ones – you could
    also use chicken or pork)
100g (3½oz) Cheddar,
    finely grated
1 egg, lightly beaten
salt and freshly ground
    black pepper

**To serve:**
your choice of favourite pickles,
    mustard and ketchup, or
    any burger relish

**YOU WILL NEED**
large baking tray, roughly
    38 x 27cm (15 x 10½in),
    lined with baking parchment
10cm (4in) cookie cutter

1   Preheat the oven to 220°C (200°C fan/425°F/Gas 7). Unroll the sheet of pastry and, using the cookie cutter, cut out 6 rounds. Slather each pastry round with 1 tablespoon of the onion jam, leaving a narrow border around the edge. Place them on a tray in the fridge until needed.

2   Using the same cookie cutter as a template, draw 6 circles onto the sheet of baking parchment, evenly spaced apart, and place drawn-side down on the baking tray.

3   Drizzle oil over the drawn circles on the lined baking tray and sprinkle with thyme. Season with salt and pepper, then scatter over the onion rings. Place a meatball in the middle of each circle and gently press it down to form a flat "burger" patty. Divide the grated cheese between the tarts, sprinkling it over the top of the smashed meatballs.

4   Drape the pastry discs, jam-side down, over the meatballs. Using the back of a fork, press around the edge of each pastry disc to seal. Score the tops in a diamond pattern with a sharp knife and then brush with egg.

5   Bake for 30–35 minutes, until the pastry is golden and crisp. Remove the tarts from the oven and allow them to sit on the tray for 5 minutes. Slide a spatula underneath each one and deftly flip them over. Dress with your choice of pickles, mustard, ketchup, or any burger relish you love.

# Upside Down Cheese & Pickle Sandwich

Picture the scene... it's late, you've made your way home after a night out with the gang, you're probably a little tipsy, and you haven't eaten. There's little food in the house, but you do have a packet of crisps, a chunk of Cheddar, and a jar of pickle that's been in the back of the fridge for a while, and, of course, if you're like me, a ubiquitous sheet of puff pastry. I present to you the puff pastry sandwich of joy!

## Serves 2

320g (11oz) sheet of ready-rolled puff pastry, roughly 35 x 23cm (14 x 9in), or use homemade (see p12)
2 tbsp sandwich pickle
drizzle of olive oil
150g (5½oz) crisps, any flavour, but I think ready-salted is the best
100g (3½oz) strong Cheddar, finely grated
1 egg, lightly beaten
salt and freshly ground black pepper

### YOU WILL NEED

large baking tray, roughly 38 x 27cm (15 x 10½in), lined with baking parchment

1 Preheat the oven to 220°C (200°C fan/425°F/Gas 7). Unroll the sheet of pastry and cut out two 14cm (5½in) squares. Spread 1 tablespoon of the sandwich pickle over each square, leaving a narrow border. Place in the fridge until needed.

2 Mark out 2 squares on the baking paper, the same size as the pastry and with space between each one, and place drawn-side down on the baking tray. Drizzle with olive oil and season with salt and pepper.

3 Take half of the crisps and scrunch them up into crumbs, then sprinkle over the drawn squares, leaving a 1cm (½in) border around the edge. Add a generous pile of cheese over the crushed crisps.

4 Lay a square of puff pastry, pickle-side down, over each pile of cheese. Using the back of a teaspoon, scallop the edges of the pastry to seal. Score the tops in a diamond pattern with a sharp knife and then brush with egg.

5 Bake for 25 minutes, until the pastry is golden and crisp. Remove the tarts from the oven and allow them to sit on the tray for 5 minutes. Lay a piece of baking parchment on top, followed by a chopping board, and carefully flip the tarts over. Remove the tray and peel off the backing paper.

6 Allow the tarts to cool for a further 5 minutes before scattering the remaining crisps over one of the pastry squares. Slide a spatula underneath the other tart and flip it over on top of the first, then press down until you hear a crunch. Slice diagonally in half to serve.

# Upside Down Mac 'n' Cheese Pie

The ultimate comfort food. Here, I'm dialling up the carbs with pasta *and* a layer of puff pastry. The trick to a good mac and cheese is to use two types of cheese. I go for something strong, like an extra-mature Cheddar, combined with a stringy, nutty cheese, such as Emmental, which works perfectly. Although, you could go with something even cheesier, like Velveeta, an American brand of melting cheese, that is sinful, but really makes a difference.

**Serves 4–6**

320g (11oz) sheet of ready-rolled puff pastry, roughly 35 x 23cm (14 x 9in), or use homemade (see p12)
200g (7oz) macaroni or spirali
1 recipe quantity of Cheese Sauce (see p14)
7 streaky bacon rashers
drizzle of olive oil
100g (3½oz) breadcrumbs
50g (1¾oz) strong Cheddar, finely grated
1 egg, lightly beaten
salt and freshly ground black pepper
chopped chives, to garnish

**YOU WILL NEED**
large baking tray, roughly 38 x 27cm (15 x 10½in), lined with baking parchment

1   Preheat the oven to 220°C (200°C fan/425°F/Gas 7). Unroll the sheet of pastry and set aside.

2   Cook the pasta in a saucepan of boiling salted water for half the time instructed on the packet. Drain well and stir the pasta into the prepared cheese sauce.

3   Meanwhile, fry the bacon in a drizzle of olive oil in a frying pan until dark and crispy. Remove the bacon from the pan, drain on kitchen paper, and chop it into small pieces. Mix the breadcrumbs with the cheese. Set aside.

4   Mark out a large rectangle on the baking parchment, the same size as the pastry, and place it drawn-side down on the baking tray. Drizzle generously with olive oil, then season with salt and pepper.

5   Leaving a 1cm (½in) border, sprinkle the cheesy breadcrumbs over the marked rectangle, then top with half of the crispy bacon. Spoon half of the mac and cheese over the bacon, making sure you keep it within the marked rectangle, then top with the rest of the bacon and the remaining mac and cheese.

6   Lay the pastry sheet over the mac and cheese. Using the back of a fork or teaspoon, press around the edges of the pastry to seal. Score the top in a diamond pattern with a sharp knife and then brush with beaten egg.

7   Bake for 25–30 minutes, until the pastry is golden and crisp. Remove the pie from the oven and allow it to sit on the tray for 10 minutes. Lay a piece of baking parchment on top, followed by a chopping board, and carefully flip the tart over in one swift move. Remove the tray and peel off the backing paper. Sprinkle with chives and cut into squares to serve.

# Chicken & Chorizo Tarte Tatin

What I love most about chorizo is the wonderful garlicky, paprika-infused fat and colour it releases when cooking. The popular Spanish sausage adds both a deep-red hue and a spicy smokiness to this savoury version of the classic tart.

**Serves 4**

320g (11oz) sheet of ready-rolled shortcrust pastry, roughly 35 x 23cm (14 x 9in), or use homemade (see p12)
200g (7oz) dry-cured chorizo sausage, cut into thick slices
3 round shallots, peeled and cut in half lengthways
1 tsp chopped thyme leaves, plus extra to serve
4 skinless, boneless chicken thighs, each cut into 4 large chunks
1 egg, lightly beaten
salt and freshly ground black pepper

**YOU WILL NEED**
20cm (8in) ovenproof skillet or cast-iron pan

1   Unroll the sheet of pastry and cut out a 23cm (9in) round; you may have to roll the pastry out slightly to ensure it is large enough. Place it in the fridge until needed.

2   Place the ovenproof skillet or pan on a medium heat. Add the chorizo and sauté for roughly 5 minutes on each side until it starts to colour and release its oil. Add the shallots, cut-side down, and scatter over half of the thyme. Cook for 5 minutes, turning halfway, until the shallots start to caramelize in the chorizo oil.

3   Next, add the chicken thighs to the pan and cook for a further 5 minutes, turning halfway, until coloured on both sides. Arrange the ingredients in the pan so you have an even spread of chicken, chorizo, and shallots. Season with salt and pepper.

4   Meanwhile, preheat the oven to 200°C (180°C fan/400°F/Gas 6).

5   Remove the pastry round from the fridge and drape it over the ingredients in the pan, then carefully tuck in the edge of the pastry. Brush the top with egg and cut a slash with a sharp knife to make a hole for the steam to escape.

6   Bake for 25 minutes, or until the pastry is darkly golden and crisp. Allow the tart to sit for 5 minutes. Place a large platter on top of the pan and carefully flip the tart over, right-side up. Lift off the pan to reveal the tart, then sprinkle the top with the remaining thyme.

# Deep-Pan Focaccia Pizza Pie

My husband, The Viking, is a fan of deep-pan pizza. I think it's his love of bread – after all, isn't this type of pizza essentially fluffy bread topped with tomato and cheese? This focaccia pizza pie is my compromise, and while it's a little time-consuming to make the dough, it's undeniably good. The deep, fluffy base can be topped with any of your favourite fresh seasonal ingredients – I've gone for one that combines my Tomato & Olive Sauce (see p14) with cavolo nero greens, and a mix of cheeses.

## Serves 4

### For the dough:
7g packet (2¼ tsp) instant dried yeast
1½ tsp fine sea salt, plus extra to season
½ tsp caster sugar
1 tbsp olive oil
300ml (10fl oz) lukewarm water
500g (1lb 2oz) strong bread flour, plus extra for dusting
extra virgin olive oil, for greasing and drizzling

### For the topping:
4–5 cavolo nero leaves, depending on size, tough stalks removed, and leaves torn into small pieces
100g (3½oz) Tomato & Olive Sauce (see p14)
150g (5½oz) mozzarella, drained and torn into pieces
50g (1¾oz) strong Cheddar, grated
100g (3½oz) mixed olives
1 tbsp dried oregano
freshly ground black pepper

### YOU WILL NEED
33 x 25cm (13 x 10in) roasting tin/dish, greased generously

1  To make the dough, place all the ingredients, except the extra virgin olive oil, in a large bowl and bring them together into a rough ball with a spatula or your hand. Tip the dough out onto a lightly oiled surface and knead for 5 minutes, until it forms a shaggy, sticky ball. (This can also be done in a stand mixer with a dough hook.)

2  Generously oil the cleaned bowl (or use a large, lidded container). Place the dough in the bowl or container, cover with a damp tea towel or lid, and leave to rest for 30 minutes. Remove the tea towel/lid and, with damp hands, press your fingers into the dough, stretching and pulling it for about a minute. Cover the bowl/container and leave the dough to rest for another 30 minutes. Repeat this three more times, then leave the dough to rest for a final 1 hour, or until doubled in size.

3  Gently tip the risen dough into the pan or tin and, using oiled fingers, press the dough out to cover the base, then press indentations over the top. Place a damp tea towel over the pan/tin and leave to prove for 30 minutes.

4  Meanwhile, preheat the oven to 220°C (200°C fan/425°F/Gas 7).

5  To top the pizza pie, steam the cavolo nero leaves until wilted. Spread the tomato and olive sauce over the focaccia base, leaving a generous border. Scatter the mozzarella, half of the Cheddar, and the cavolo nero over, then top with the olives and the remaining Cheddar. Using oiled fingers, gently press more indentations into the dough.

6  Sprinkle over the oregano and season with salt and plenty of pepper. Bake for 25 minutes, or until the crust is golden and puffy, and the cheese is wonderfully gooey. Lift the pizza out of the pan/tin and serve cut into slices.

# Cottage Pie with Carrot, Swede & Potato Topping

I've upped the veg quota in this cottage pie by adding swede and carrot to the mashed potato topping, which adds a different flavour dimension to the classic recipe. This is perfect warming, comfort food in one dish – all that's needed is to place the pie in the centre of the table and let everyone help themselves.

**Serves 4**

## For the filling:

50g (1¾oz) salted butter
2 tbsp olive oil
1 onion, finely chopped
2 celery sticks, finely chopped
1 carrot, finely chopped
2 garlic cloves, grated
1 tsp chopped rosemary leaves
1 tsp chopped thyme leaves
300g (10oz) minced beef
1 tsp tomato paste
400g (14oz) can chopped
    tomatoes
500ml (16fl oz) vegetable stock
4 tsp gravy powder
100ml (3½fl oz) white wine
100g (3½oz) frozen peas
salt and freshly ground pepper

## For the topping:

1kg (2¼lb) potatoes for
    mashing, such as Maris
    Piper or russet, peeled and
    cut into large chunks
1 swede, peeled and
    finely chopped
2 large carrots, finely chopped
50g (1¾oz) salted butter
100g (3½oz) Cheddar, grated

**YOU WILL NEED**
large, oval baking/pie dish

1 Preheat the oven to 200°C (180°C fan/400°F/Gas 6).

2 To make the filling, melt the butter and olive oil in a sauté pan on a medium heat. Add the onion, celery, and carrot, and sauté for 5 minutes, until softened. Stir in the garlic and herbs and cook for an additional 5 minutes, stirring regularly to prevent the garlic from burning. Season with a little salt and pepper.

3 Add the mince and cook, stirring to break up any large clumps, for 6 minutes, or until it begins to brown. Stir in the tomato paste, canned tomatoes, stock, gravy powder, and wine. Bring to a gentle boil, then turn the heat down to low. Add the peas and gently simmer away for 15 minutes, until the sauce has reduced and thickened.

4 Meanwhile, make the mash. I like to steam the vegetables because it creates a fluffier, less watery mash. Add the chopped veg to a tiered steamer (I put the swede in the bottom steamer basket, as it takes longer to cook, and the potatoes and carrots on top). Steam the vegetables for 10 minutes, until tender, then tip them into a large bowl, place a tea-towel over the top, and leave for 2 minutes – this will help to steam-dry them, ensuring a fluffy mash. Add the butter and mash well, then mix in the Cheddar. Season with salt and pepper.

5 Tip the filling into the baking or pie dish and carefully spoon the mash mix on top. Fork over to rough up the top (adding a few extra knobs of butter, if you like) and bake for 30 minutes, or until gloriously golden.

**Cook's Tip:**
You can prepare the mash up to 2 days in advance and keep it in the fridge. Alternatively, freeze for up to 3 months and defrost before use.

# Prosecco Fish Pie

I absolutely love a fish pie, but I wanted to elevate it to a special occasion dish. It's not just the combination of salmon, prawns, and smoked haddock, or the golden potato topping that makes this pie so exceptional, it's the creamy Prosecco sauce that takes it to another fabulous level. There's something about the floral, fruity, citrus notes that just works, turning this humble favourite into a feast for friends.

**Serves 4**

**For the potato topping:**
1 tbsp olive oil
40g (1½oz) salted butter
5 large potatoes, diced
1 garlic clove, chopped
1 tsp thyme leaves

**For the filling:**
400g (14oz) skinless smoked
   haddock or cod
250g (9oz) skinless salmon
   fillets
500ml (16fl oz) whole milk
100ml (3½fl oz) Prosecco DOC
50g (1¾oz) salted butter
50g (1¾oz) plain flour
100g (3½oz) Cheddar, finely
   grated
1 tsp Dijon mustard
100g (3½oz) frozen peas
175g (6oz) large, raw peeled
   prawns
salt and freshly ground
   black pepper
chopped chives, to garnish
green salad, to serve

**YOU WILL NEED**
large ovenproof pie dish

1   To make the potato topping, place a large sauté pan (with a lid) on a medium heat and add the olive oil and butter. Add the potatoes, garlic, and thyme. Cover the pan with the lid, turn the heat to low and steam-cook the potatoes for 8 minutes, until tender. Remove the lid, turn up the heat and sauté until the potatoes turn a gentle golden colour. Remove the potatoes from the pan and set aside.

2   Put the haddock and salmon in the sauté pan and pour over the milk. Cover with the lid, turn the heat to medium and bring to a simmer. When the milk starts to bubble, turn the heat off and let the fish poach for 3 minutes. Gently remove the fish with a spatula (it should be slightly undercooked at this point), leaving the milk in the pan. Set aside the fish.

3   Place the pan containing the milk (there should be around 400ml/14fl oz) back on a medium heat. Pour in the Prosecco and mix in the butter and flour. Whisk gently for roughly 5 minutes until the butter melts and the sauce has thickened to a creamy consistency. Turn the heat to low and simmer gently for another 3 minutes, stirring occasionally. Stir in the Cheddar and mustard, then season with salt and pepper. Remove the pan from the heat and stir in the peas and prawns.

4   Preheat the oven to 190°C (170°C fan/375°F/Gas 5). Flake the poached salmon and haddock in large chunks into the large ovenproof dish. Pour the Prosecco sauce over and gently mix until combined. Spoon the golden chunky potatoes on top. Bake for 15–20 minutes, until the potatoes turn crisp and a darker shade of golden. Serve with a sprinkling of fresh chopped chives and a green salad.

# Steak, Ale & Shallot Pie

Pies remind me of cosy nights by the fire, being with family and loved ones, and act as a reminder to take things more slowly. They evoke feelings of nostalgia and comfort. This pie, with its caramelized shallot and potato topping, is a celebration of slower days, when the world can wait and we can all get together to enjoy a delicious meal.

**Serves 4**

2 tbsp plain flour
1kg (2¼lb) beef shin, cut into
    large chunks
2 tbsp olive oil, plus extra for
    the potatoes
40g (1½oz) salted butter
400g (14oz) shallots, peeled
    and halved lengthways
1 tbsp thyme leaves
1 tsp chopped rosemary leaves
2 garlic cloves, crushed
200ml (7fl oz) dark ale
400ml (14fl oz) beef stock
500g (1lb 2oz) baby new
    potatoes, thickly sliced
    into rounds
salt and freshly ground
    black pepper
green beans, to serve

**YOU WILL NEED**
large ovenproof pie dish

1   Start to make the filling. Place the flour in a large bowl and season with salt and pepper. Add the beef and turn to coat it in the seasoned flour.

2   Place a large sauté pan (with a lid) on a medium heat. Add half of the olive oil and half of the butter to the pan with the beef and cook for roughly 5 minutes, turning occasionally, until browned all over. Remove from the pan with a slotted spoon onto a plate and set aside.

3   Add most of the remaining oil and butter to the pan with half of the shallots and cook for roughly 5 minutes, turning regularly. Add half of the thyme and cook for another 5 minutes, until the shallots are dark golden. Remove the shallots and set aside (these will be for the topping). Repeat with the remaining shallots and thyme, adding more oil and butter, if needed.

4   Return the browned beef to the pan containing half of the cooked golden shallots. Stir in the rosemary and garlic, and after a minute, add the ale and stock. Bring up to boiling point, then turn the heat down to low, cover with the lid, and let the stew gently bubble away for 1 hour.

5   Meanwhile, par-boil the potatoes in a large saucepan of boiling salted water for 4 minutes, until softened but not fully cooked. Drain the potatoes well, then return them to the pan and douse in olive oil. Season with salt and pepper.

6   Preheat the oven to 190°C (170°C fan/375°F/Gas 5). Tip the pie filling into the large ovenproof pie dish. Arrange the slices of potato and the reserved shallots on top (I like to do it with a ring of potatoes and then a ring of shallots, starting from the middle to the outer edge). Bake for 20 minutes, or until the top is golden and starting to crisp. Serve with green beans.

# Upside Down Ratatouille Tart

I love experimenting with traditional dishes, especially if it allows me to use up what's left over in the fridge. With this dish, I'm drifting slightly from the classic and substituting red pepper with beetroot as that's what I had to hand. I genuinely believe that you use what you can, and that's how we evolve in the food world. You'll need my luscious Tomato & Olive Sauce for this (see p14).

## Serves 6

320g (11oz) sheet of ready-rolled puff pastry, roughly 35 x 23cm (14 x 9in), or use homemade (see p12)
3 tbsp olive oil
50g (1¾oz) salted butter
1 tsp oregano leaves, plus extra to garnish
1 tsp thyme leaves
1 tsp rosemary leaves
2 tsp sweet smoked paprika
finely grated zest of ½ unwaxed lemon
1 long potato, cut into roughly 5mm (¼in) thick slices
2 medium raw beetroots, cut into roughly 1cm (½in) slices
1 yellow courgette, cut into roughly 1cm (½in) slices
1 green courgette, cut into roughly 1cm (½in) slices
2 red onions, cut into roughly 1cm (½in) slices
150g (5½oz) Tomato & Olive Sauce (see p14)
1 egg, lightly beaten
salt and freshly ground black pepper

### YOU WILL NEED
large baking tray, 38 x 27cm (15 x 10½in), lined with baking parchment

1　Preheat the oven to 180°C (160°C fan/375°F/Gas 7). Unroll the sheet of pastry and set aside.

2　Mark out a large rectangle on the baking paper, the same size as the pastry, and place it drawn-side down on the baking tray. Drizzle generously with half of the olive oil and dot all over with small knobs of butter. Sprinkle with the oregano, thyme, and rosemary, followed by a dusting of paprika. Scatter over the lemon zest.

3　Leaving a 2cm (½in) border, arrange the vegetables in four overlapping rows within the drawn rectangle on the baking paper. Each row should butt up against the next one, without overlapping. (You can arrange the vegetables randomly or in groups, depending on your preference.) Season with salt and pepper, and drizzle over the remaining olive oil.

4　Carefully spoon the tomato and olive sauce over – little dollops of sauce spread with the back of a spoon will help to ensure you don't move the rows of vegetables.

5　Drape the pastry carefully over the sauce-topped veg. Using the back of a fork or teaspoon, press around the edges of the pastry to seal. Score the top in a diamond pattern with a sharp knife and then brush with egg.

6　Bake for 40 minutes, or until the pastry is golden and crisp. Remove the tart from the oven and allow it to sit on the tray for 10 minutes. Lay a piece of baking parchment on top, followed by a chopping board, and carefully flip the tart over in one swift move. Remove the tray and peel off the backing paper. Scatter over a few oregano leaves and cut into portions to serve.

# Mushroom & Leek Monkey Crust Pie

Autumn is all about warming, comfort food. And this pie is the king of comfort – with its filling of wild mushrooms, woody herbs, and leeks it's a celebration of the season. The monkey crust pie topping is perfect for using up any leftover bits of pastry you may have lingering in the fridge or freezer.

## Serves 4

1 tbsp olive oil
50g (1¾oz) salted butter
3 banana shallots, chopped
1 large leek, chopped
350g (12oz) mixed wild mushrooms, sliced
1 tsp chopped rosemary leaves
1 tsp chopped thyme leaves
1 tbsp chopped chives
2 x 320g (11oz) sheets of puff pastry, roughly 35 x 23cm (14 x 9in), or 1 sheet plus leftovers, or use homemade (see p12)
1 egg, lightly beaten
steamed veg, to serve (optional)

### For the creamy mustard sauce:
500ml (16fl oz) whole milk
50g (1¾oz) plain flour
50g (1¾oz) salted butter
2 tbsp white wine
100g (3½oz) vintage Gouda, finely grated
1 tsp Dijon mustard
salt and freshly ground black pepper

### YOU WILL NEED
20cm (8in) round pie dish, greased with butter

1 Preheat the oven to 190°C (170°C fan/375°F/Gas 5).

2 To make the creamy mustard sauce, pour the milk into a saucepan on a medium heat, then add the flour and butter. Using a balloon whisk, gently whisk the sauce for about 3 minutes, until it begins to thicken. Stir in the white wine and continue to cook, whisking, for another 3 minutes. Turn the heat to its lowest setting and cook the sauce for a further 5 minutes, whisking occasionally, to prevent it catching on the bottom, until thick and creamy. Take the pan off the heat and stir the Gouda and mustard into the sauce. Season with a little salt and pepper, to taste, then set aside.

3 Heat the olive oil and butter in a large sauté pan on a medium heat. Add the shallots and sauté for 3 minutes, or until they start to soften. Stir in the leek and sauté gently for another 5 minutes, until softened. Add the mushrooms and herbs to the pan, stir, cover with the lid, and cook for 6 minutes. The mushrooms should release their liquid and soften. Remove the lid, turn the heat up a little, season with salt and plenty of pepper, and sauté until the mushrooms take on a golden colour and the liquid has evaporated. Pour the creamy mustard sauce into the pan and stir until combined. Leave the sauce to cool while you prepare the crust.

4 Unroll one of the pastry sheets and place it in the greased pie dish. Trim the edges, ensuring you leave a 2cm (¾in) overhang, then brush the edge with water. Pour in the cooled, creamy leek and mushroom filling.

5 Unroll (or roll out) the remaining pastry and cut it into small squares, each roughly 5 x 5cm (2 x 2in). Randomly arrange the squares over the filling until the top of the pie is covered. Crimp the edge of the pie to join the top and base. Brush with egg and bake for 40 minutes, or until the pastry is golden and crisp. Cut into slices and serve with steamed veg, if you like.

# Upside Down Banana PB&J

The first time I had a toasted sandwich made in a proper sandwich toaster was in the early '80s, and I was at my friend Gabby's house. Her mum made a peanut butter and jam sandwich, and I think my mind melted with excitement. My upside-down version is more of a naughty midnight feast than something you'd eat for lunch or dinner, but it's well worth turning the oven on for!

**Serves 2**

320g (11oz) sheet of ready-rolled puff pastry, roughly 35 x 23cm (14 x 9in), or use homemade (see p12)
4 tbsp peanut butter, crunchy or smooth
3 tbsp runny honey
75g (2½oz) raspberries
75g (2½oz) blueberries
1 banana, cut into slices
1 egg, lightly beaten

**YOU WILL NEED**
large baking tray, roughly 38 x 27cm (15 x 10½in), lined with baking parchment

1 Preheat the oven to 220°C (200°C fan/425°F/Gas 7). Unroll the sheet of pastry and cut out two 14cm (5½in) squares. Spread 2 tablespoons of the peanut butter over each square, leaving a narrow border. Place in the fridge until needed.

2 Mark out 2 squares on the baking parchment, the same size as the pastry and with space between each one, and place drawn-side down on the baking tray. Drizzle the honey over the marked squares.

3 Arrange the raspberries and blueberries on top of one of the squares, leaving a 1cm (½in) border. Place the banana slices on the second pastry square, leaving a narrow border.

4 Lay a square of puff pastry, peanut butter-side down, over each pile of fruit. Using the back of a teaspoon, scallop the edges of each pastry square to seal. Score the tops in a diamond pattern with a sharp knife and then brush with egg.

5 Bake for 25 minutes, until the pastry is golden and crisp. Remove the tarts from the oven and allow them to sit on the tray for 5 minutes. Lay a piece of baking parchment on top, followed by a chopping board, and carefully flip the tarts over in one swift move. Remove the tray and peel off the backing paper. Allow to cool for a further 5 minutes.

6 Slide a spatula underneath one of the squares and flip it over on top of the second square to make the ultimate BPB&J! Slice diagonally in half to serve.

# Dinner Party Feasts

I remained in London while at university, and spent the first year living at home with Mum. I'm not sure if she was expecting typical student behaviour from me – staggering home drunk at 3am or holding banging house parties in the garage – but she certainly didn't get that. Instead, I spent evenings hosting dinner parties for my eclectic art foundation friends. Yes, there was a lot of wine, and while there may have been a pile of dishes left in the sink, and a pile of sleeping bodies on sofas in the morning, it was all very well behaved. The food was often experimental, but there was always a lot of it: three proper courses, with sides, and cocktails, and wine. It was all very suburban sit-com, but delightful and civilized, and it's what I still like to do to this day. In this chapter, I'm sharing three different dinner party menus that will keep everyone happy, including a traditional Jewish Friday night dinner.

*Chopped Liver with Poppy & Fennel Seed Crackers • Roast Chicken • Upside Down Cauliflower Cheese Tart • Chocolate Chestnut Roulade*

Growing up, Friday night dinners were always a big deal at our house. While Mum was keen to encourage my brother and I to take an active interest in religion, we were there for the food. And the food was good. Mum always cooked the classics: a starter of chopped liver, followed by roast chicken with all the trimmings, usually cauli cheese, and finishing off with some kind of dessert, often served with a fruit salad. I've recreated it here with a few upside-down twists.

## Chopped Liver with Poppy & Fennel Seed Crackers
**SERVES 4–6 (AS A CANAPÉ OR STARTER)**

With all the reverence this dish carries in the Jewish community, you'd have thought it was complicated to make or included rare ingredients. Yet it's unbelievably simple, if not downright basic. It would originally have been made with schmaltz (rendered chicken or goose fat) but unless you've recently roasted a bird, I think it's a step too far. I prefer a combination of olive oil and butter.

3 large eggs
50g (1¾oz) salted butter
1 tbsp olive oil
1 white onion, finely chopped
400g (14oz) chicken livers, veiny bits trimmed, if preferred
salt and freshly ground black pepper
Poppy & Fennel Seed Crackers (see p51) or toast, or your choice of crackers, to serve

1   Hard-boil the eggs in a small saucepan of boiling water for 10 minutes, then peel and set aside to cool.

2   Heat the butter and oil in a large, shallow frying pan on a medium heat. Once the butter has melted, add the onion and sauté gently until soft and just beginning to colour.

3   Turn the heat up to medium–high, add the livers to the pan and fry, stirring occasionally, for about 8 minutes, until cooked with a touch of pink in the middle. (Many people cook their livers all the way through, which is also fine; the pâté will just be a bit drier and coarser.) Season with plenty of salt and pepper – the livers can take it! Set aside to cool slightly.

4   Cut the eggs in half and set aside one half of an egg, then add the remaining eggs and cooked liver mixture to a food processor and blitz until finely chopped. You don't want it to be too smooth. Transfer the mixture to a shallow serving dish and grate the remaining egg over the top.

5   Place the pâté in the fridge to settle for at least 1 hour, or it can be made up to 1 day in advance and stored in an airtight container in the fridge. Serve with Poppy & Fennel Seed Crackers.

## Roast Chicken
### MAIN (SERVES 4)

It may seem odd to include a recipe for such a classic, but sometimes they are the ones most often forgotten, or at least set aside, for new, trendy dishes. This is a classic for good reason – Friday night dinner roast chicken is the best. You'd better agree, or my mum will come for you! Serve it with all your favourite sides and trimmings.

1.5kg (3lb 3oz) free-range chicken
1 large onion, sliced into wedges
2 celery sticks, chopped
1 carrot, chopped
3 garlic cloves, left whole
    and unpeeled
few sprigs each of rosemary and/or thyme
150ml (5fl oz) white wine
salt and freshly ground
    black pepper

### For the herb butter:
100g (3½oz) salted butter, softened
1 tsp chopped rosemary
1 tsp chopped thyme

### YOU WILL NEED
large roasting tin

1   Preheat the oven to 180°C (160°C fan/350°F/Gas 4). To prepare the chicken (and for the ultimate crispy skin), place the bird in a large bowl in the sink. Pour over enough just-boiled water from a kettle to cover, then leave the chicken for a few minutes while you prepare the vegetables.

2   Spread half of the onion wedges along with all the celery, carrot, and garlic over the bottom of the roasting tin. Carefully lift the chicken out of the hot water and lay it on top of the veg, breast-side up. Stuff the rest of the onion inside the cavity along with the rosemary and/or thyme sprigs.

3   To make the herb butter, mix all the ingredients in a bowl until combined. Slide your fingers gently under the chicken skin to separate it from the breast. Take half of the herb butter and push it under the skin in an even layer, then spread the rest over the top of the chicken.

4   Turn the chicken over so it's breast-side down. Season the bottom of the chicken with salt and pepper and pour the white wine into the tin. Place the chicken in the oven and roast for 1 hour, then remove from the oven.

5   Increase the oven temperature to 200°C (180°C fan/400°F/Gas 6). Using two forks, turn the chicken over, breast-side-up, and pop it back in the oven for a final 30–45 minutes, or until the skin is a glorious golden brown. To check the chicken is cooked, gently pull one leg away from the body and puncture the flesh in the crevice between the leg and the breast – the juices should run clear. If it's cloudy or a little bloody, then put the chicken back in the oven for a further few minutes.

6   Once the chicken is out of the oven, cover it with foil and a tea towel and set it aside to rest, while the cauli cheese tart bakes (see p113).

### Cook's Note:
I always buy a medium-sized chicken, irrespective of how many people I'm cooking for (a medium bird will feed 4 people with nothing left on the bones). If you have more than 4 guests (or want leftovers), I recommend buying 2 medium chickens and roasting them side-by-side in a large roasting tin (this is so much nicer than buying a larger bird). Leftover, cooked chicken will keep for up to 3 days in the fridge.

# Upside Down Cauliflower Cheese Tart

**SIDE (SERVES 4–6)**

Cauliflower cheese was my mum's go-to side dish. It wouldn't be a Friday night dinner without it. This version uses all the classic components but in a delicious tart form.

320g (11oz) sheet of ready-rolled puff pastry, roughly 35 x 23cm (14 x 9in), or use homemade (see p12)
1 tbsp Dijon mustard
drizzle of olive oil
1 tsp thyme leaves
100g (3½oz) breadcrumbs
100g (3½oz) strong Cheddar, grated
1 cauliflower, leaves removed, cut into small florets
200ml (7fl oz) Cheese Sauce (made with Cheddar, see p14), left to cool slightly
1 egg, lightly beaten
salt and freshly ground black pepper
few small sprigs of rosemary, to garnish

**YOU WILL NEED**
large baking tray, roughly 38 x 27cm (15 x 10½in), lined with baking parchment

1   While the chicken is roasting in the oven, unroll the sheet of pastry and spread the mustard over one side, leaving a narrow border. Place in the fridge until needed.

2   Mark out a large rectangle on the baking parchment, the same size as the pastry, and place it drawn-side down on the baking tray. Drizzle generously with olive oil and sprinkle with the thyme. Season with salt and pepper.

3   Leaving a 1cm (½in) border, sprinkle the breadcrumbs over the seasoned oil on the marked rectangle, followed by the grated Cheddar. Arrange the cauliflower florets on top in an even layer, then pour the slightly cooled cheese sauce over.

4   Lay the pastry, mustard-side down, over the cauliflower cheese. Using the back of a teaspoon, scallop the edges of the pastry to seal. Score the top in a diamond pattern with a sharp knife and then brush with beaten egg.

5   Bake at 200°C (180°C fan/400°F/Gas 6) for 25–30 minutes, until the pastry is golden and crisp. Remove the tart from the oven and allow it to sit on the tray for 5 minutes. Lay a piece of baking parchment on top of the pie, followed by a chopping board, and carefully flip it over. Remove the tray and peel off the backing paper. Slice into squares and scatter over a few sprigs of rosemary. Serve with the roast chicken, sides, and trimmings of your choice.

# Chocolate Chestnut Roulade
## DESSERT (SERVES 4 WITH LEFTOVERS)

A roulade may be considered a tricky option when it comes to dinner-party desserts, but Mum's version is pretty much fail-safe, partly because it's supposed to look crumbly, cracked, and messy! I realize, as I write, that this could have been what she told us to save face, but either way, I love the way it looks, and it reminds me of Mum, and that's the most important thing.

### For the sponge:
4 large eggs, separated
125g (4½oz) caster sugar
150g (5½oz) good-quality plain chocolate
    (at least 75% cocoa solids), broken
    into even-sized pieces
1½ tbsp hot water

### For the filling:
300ml (10fl oz) double or whipping cream
250g (9oz) can crème de marron
    (sweet chestnut spread)

### YOU WILL NEED
large 34 x 24cm (13½ x 9½in) Swiss roll
    tin, lined with foil or baking parchment,
    greased well with butter

1   Preheat the oven to 170°C (150°C fan/340°F/ Gas 3½). In a large bowl, beat the egg yolks with the sugar until pale and creamy.

2   Melt the chocolate (I do this gradually in a microwave or use the classic heatproof bowl set over a pan of simmering water method). When melted, add the hot water, then gently stir the melted chocolate into the egg and sugar mixture.

3   Using an electric hand whisk, beat the egg whites to stiff peaks and then gently fold them into the chocolate mixture. Pour it into the lined tin, spreading it out evenly to cover the base. Bake for 20 minutes, then reduce the temperature to 120°C (100°C fan/ 200°F/Gas ¼) and bake the sponge for a further 10 minutes, until risen and springy.

4   Meanwhile, grease another sheet of foil or baking parchment, slightly larger than the Swiss roll tin, and place it on a flat surface or large board where it won't need to be moved for a while (around 8 hours).

5   Now the tricky bit. When the sponge is ready, take the tin out of the oven and immediately turn it over onto the greased foil/paper. Leave the sponge, with the tin still on top, for at least 8 hours. I tend to bake it in the morning, then get on with life, or bake it in the evening and leave it to sit overnight.

6   To make the filling/topping, whisk the cream to a soft, light, whippy consistency in a large bowl. Gently fold in the chestnut spread until combined.

7   Remove the tin covering the sponge and carefully peel off the foil/paper backing. Spread the cream mixture evenly over the sponge. Starting at one of the short ends, using the foil/paper to help you, roll the sponge into a roulade – don't worry about any cracks or breaks, this is all part of the look. Carefully place the roulade on a serving plate and cut into slices to serve.

*Upside Down Smoked Mackerel & Tomato Tart · Slow Roast Lamb with Herby Potatoes and Veg · Upside Down Carrot, Honey & Thyme Tarte Tatin · Build-your-own Summer Berry Trifle Cocktails*

When I'm entertaining my friends, I want there to be an abundance of food, but I also want the meal to be easy. I'd rather spend time with them than be stuck in the kitchen. All the dishes in this menu look after themselves, by which I mean there's very little prep, and they're supposed to be served family-style at the table, so everyone can just dig in.

## Upside Down Smoked Mackerel & Tomato Tart

**SERVES 4–6**

The combo of smoky mackerel with sun-dried tomato cream cheese makes the perfect filling for this puff pastry tart. I love the idea of placing it upside down in the centre of the table, and once everyone takes their seats, flipping it over to do the big reveal, and then letting everyone tear in. Like a proper bacchanalian feast!

320g (11oz) sheet of ready-rolled puff pastry, roughly 35 x 23cm (14 x 9in), or use homemade (see p12)
200g (7oz) cream cheese
100g (3½oz) smoked sun-dried tomatoes in oil, drained, reserving 1 tbsp of the oil
drizzle of olive oil
1 tbsp roughly chopped dill
3 smoked mackerel fillets, skin removed, and portioned into 9 bite-sized pieces
1 egg, lightly beaten
salt and freshly ground black pepper

**YOU WILL NEED**
large baking tray, roughly 38 x 27cm (15 x 10½in), lined with baking parchment

1  Preheat the oven to 220°C (200°C fan/425°F/ Gas 7). Unroll the sheet of pastry and set aside until needed.

2  Place the cream cheese and sun-dried tomatoes with their oil in a food processor, then blitz until smooth. Set aside.

3  Drizzle the lined baking tray generously with olive oil and sprinkle with the dill. Season with salt and pepper.

4  Arrange the smoked mackerel pieces evenly spaced apart on the lined baking tray (3 rows of 3). Top the mackerel with a teaspoon of the cream cheese mixture.

5  Carefully drape the pastry over the cream cheese-topped mackerel. Press the pastry down between the pieces of mackerel until you can see nine defined mounds of fish, then seal in the filling with a fork. Press around the edges of the whole pastry sheet to seal. Score the top in a diamond pattern with a sharp knife and then brush with egg.

6  Bake for 25–30 minutes, until the pastry is golden and crisp. Remove the tart from the oven and allow it to sit on the tray for 5 minutes. Lay a piece of baking parchment on top, followed by a chopping board, and carefully flip it over. Remove the tray and peel off the backing paper. When ready to serve (it can be served hot or cold), allow your guests to pull the tart apart or slice into portions.

## Slow-Roast Lamb with Herby Potatoes and Veg
**MAIN (SERVES 4–6)**

Last summer, while on the glorious island of Mallorca, we were invited to our friend's place for lunch. Antonia and Pepe are true Mallorquins, proud of their wonderful home and all that the island produces. Pepe cooked us what I can only describe as the best roast lamb I've ever eaten. Slow roasted, along with potatoes, garlic, and rosemary, in their traditional outdoor oven; it couldn't have been simpler or more delicious, and he very kindly gave me his recipe so that I can share it with you. Cooked until falling off the bone, the lamb must be eaten to be believed – a true feast for friends.

4 potatoes, such as Maris Piper, cut into
   bite-sized chunks
3 carrots, cut into bite-sized chunks
5 shallots, quartered
250g (9oz) vine cherry tomatoes
3–4 garlic cloves, depending on size,
   left whole
drizzle of olive oil
3 rosemary sprigs
1.85kg (4lb) half leg of lamb
300ml (10fl oz) white wine

**For the rub:**
1 garlic clove, peeled
2 tsp chopped rosemary leaves
2 tsp chopped thyme leaves
1 tsp dried oregano
splash of olive oil
salt and freshly ground black pepper

**YOU WILL NEED**
large roasting tin with tight-fitting
   lid or foil

**1** Preheat the oven to 220°C (200°C fan/425°F/ Gas 7). Start with the rub. Blitz the garlic with the herbs and a splash of olive oil in a mini food processor to a chunky paste. Season with salt and pepper. Set aside.

**2** Put the potatoes, carrots, shallots, tomatoes, and whole garlic cloves in a large roasting tin, drizzle over a little olive oil and place the rosemary sprigs and leg of lamb on top. Rub the lamb all over with the garlic rub, then roast in the oven for 30 minutes, until browned all over.

**3** Carefully remove the tin from the oven, pour the white wine over the lamb and vegetables and put the lid on, making sure it's tight-fitting (or cover with foil – I used both). Reduce the heat to 180°C (160°C fan/350°F/Gas 4). Place the roasting tin back in the oven and cook for 4½ hours.

**4** At this point, remove the lid/foil and turn the oven back up to 220°C (200°C fan/425°F/ Gas 7) for a final 20-minute blast. By now, the lamb should be starting to fall off the bone with crispy bits around the edges, and the veg and garlic gloriously soft and golden. Remove the tin from the oven.

**5** Using 2 forks, shred the roast lamb off the bone in chunks. Serve the shredded lamb on top of the roasted veg and garlic with the lamb juices spooned over.

## Upside Down Carrot, Honey & Thyme Tarte Tatin
### SIDE (SERVES 4–6)

Honey-glazed carrots go beautifully with roasted meats, especially lamb, and work well as a topping in this savoury puff pastry tarte tartin. It takes a little effort to arrange the carrots, but it's worth it for the finished result.

320g (11oz) sheet of ready-rolled puff pastry, roughly 35 x 23cm (14 x 9in), or use homemade (see p12)
2 tbsp chilli jam
drizzle of olive oil
drizzle of runny honey, plus extra to serve
75g (2½oz) salted butter, cut into small pieces
2 thyme sprigs, leaves picked
4 large carrots, cut into rounds no thicker than a pound coin
1 egg, lightly beaten
salt and freshly ground black pepper

### YOU WILL NEED
large baking tray, roughly 38 x 27cm (15 x 10½in), lined with baking parchment
22cm (8½in) diameter round plate

1  Preheat the oven to 200°C (180°C fan/400°F/ Gas 6). Unroll the sheet of pastry. Using the 22cm (8½in) round plate as a template, cut the pastry into a disc. Slather the chilli jam over one side of the pastry, leaving a narrow border. Place in the fridge until needed.

2  Draw around the same plate onto the baking parchment, then place it drawn-side down on the baking tray. Drizzle a little olive oil and honey over the marked round, then dot the butter on top. Finish with a sprinkling of thyme, saving some to serve, and season with salt and pepper.

3  Place one large carrot round in the centre of the baking paper circle, then working your way outwards, place the carrot slices in overlapping rings around the central slice. Start with the larger rounds in the centre, making sure you leave a 2cm (¾in) border around the outer edge – you should have at least 5 rings of overlapping carrot slices. Season with extra salt and pepper.

4  Lay the pastry disc over the top of the carrots. Using the back of a fork, press around the edge of the pastry to seal. Score the top in a diamond pattern with a sharp knife and then brush with egg.

5  Bake for 30 minutes, or until the pastry is golden and crisp. Remove the tart from the oven and allow it to sit on the tray for 5 minutes. Lay a piece of baking parchment on top, followed by a chopping board or plate, and carefully flip it over. Remove the tray and peel off the backing paper. Finish with a sprinkling of the reserved thyme and a drizzle of honey. Serve cut into slices as a side to the roasted lamb, potatoes, and veg.

## Build-Your-Own Summer Berry Trifle Cocktails
**DESSERT (SERVES 6)**

I love the idea of placing the various elements of this trifle on the table, and allowing guests to build their own dessert. All the essential ingredients are here, plus a selection of spirits and cordials so people can go as boozy (or not) as they like. I've cheated and used ready-made custard and cake, but if you have the time and inclination, feel free to make your own. I've also used summer berries, but you can use any seasonal fruit your heart desires.

300ml (10fl oz) whipping cream
200g (7oz) vanilla sponge cake, cut into
     small cubes
selection of alcohol, such as sherry, Aperol,
     or flavoured vodka
selection of fruit cordials, diluted with
     water, to taste
selection of jams
300ml (10fl oz) cold vanilla custard
200g (7oz) blueberries
200g (7oz) raspberries
200g (7oz) strawberries, halved or
     quartered, if large
200g (7oz) blackberries
6 cherries (optional)

### YOU WILL NEED
6 classic knickerbocker glory glasses, or
     clear glass bowls (it's nice to be able to
     see the layers of trifle)

1   Using an electric hand whisk, whip the cream in a large bowl to soft, light peaks. Place the bowl on your dining table or worktop with all the other ingredients listed in separate bottles and bowls. You'll also need plenty of spoons.

2   Let your guests build their own trifles: I would suggest starting with a few cubes of cake and a splash or two of liquid (alcoholic or diluted cordial) to let it soak into the sponge. Add a layer of jam, custard, and fruit – choose your own favourite combinations.

3   Finish each trifle with a generous topping of softly whipped cream, then pop a cherry on top, if you like. Enjoy!

# If Tarts Be the Food of Love

*Salt & Pepper Bang Bang Cauliflower Love Bites • Upside Down "Marry Me" Chicken Tart with Roasted Garlic & Parmesan Greens • Upside Down Banana & Custard Tart*

When I first met my husband (The Viking), I wanted to impress him with my cooking skills, but little did I know what I was taking on. It's not that he's a fussy eater, but he likes what he likes, and has an innate inability to try something new. I thought a twist on duck à l'orange (he wasn't vegetarian at the time) would be an impressive first meal. Let's just say that it didn't go down too well. Since then, we don't do romantic meals, but if we did, this small feast would be on the menu.

## Salt & Pepper Bang Bang Cauliflower Love Bites
### STARTER (SERVES 2)

I know it's utterly juvenile of me to include a dish called bang bang in a romantic meal for two, but I couldn't resist! These cauli bites are so delicious and fun to eat, especially if you serve them to each other dipped in something sweet and saucy. You can cook them in an air fryer or the oven.

90g (3¼oz) plain flour
175ml (6fl oz) half milk/half Greek yogurt, stirred well
½ tbsp sea salt flakes
4 tsp freshly ground black pepper, plus extra to season
1 tbsp finely grated unwaxed lemon zest
150g (5½oz) breadcrumbs
1 cauliflower, chopped into bite-sized chunks/florets
1 tbsp finely chopped chives

### For the bang bang glaze:
juice of 3 unwaxed lemons
3 tbsp runny honey
1 tbsp soy sauce
1 tsp cornstarch mixed with 1 tsp water

**YOU WILL NEED**
large baking tray, roughly 38 x 27cm (15 x 10½in), lined with baking parchment (if using the oven and not an air fryer)

1   Preheat your air fryer to 180°C (350°F) or oven to 200°C (180°C fan/400°F/Gas 6).

2   Using a balloon whisk, mix the flour, milk/yogurt, salt, 3 teaspoons of the black pepper, and the lemon zest in a large bowl to make a batter. Add the breadcrumbs to a second large bowl.

3   Add the cauliflower to the batter mixture and use a spoon to turn it until coated. Transfer the cauliflower to the breadcrumbs and turn to coat each piece in the crumbs.

4   Cook in the air fryer for 15 minutes, or place on the lined baking tray and bake in the oven for 25 minutes, until golden and crisp.

5   Meanwhile, make the glaze. Warm all the ingredients in a small pan with the remaining black pepper, stirring, until thick and glossy.

6   When the cauliflower bites are ready, toss them in the glaze, then return them to the air fryer or oven for a final 5 minutes, until glossy and sticky. Sprinkle over the chives and serve.

## Upside Down "Marry Me" Chicken Tart with Roasted Garlic & Parmesan Greens
### MAIN (SERVES 2 WITH LEFTOVERS)

"Marry Me" chicken was an internet sensation; the idea behind the dish is that it's so good it could lead to a marriage proposal! Both impressive and ridiculously easy to make, this upside-down tart is a play on the original.

320g (11oz) sheet of ready-rolled puff pastry, roughly 35 x 23cm (14 x 9in), or use homemade (see p12)
5 asparagus stalks, each cut in half
drizzle of olive oil
1 tsp dried oregano
½ tsp chilli flakes
200g (7oz) leftover roast chicken, shredded
1 egg, lightly beaten

### For the "Marry Me" sauce:
250ml (9fl oz) milk of choice
25g (scant 1oz) plain flour
25g (scant 1oz) lightly salted butter
1 garlic clove, crushed
1½ tsp sun-dried tomato paste
75g (2½oz) Parmesan, finely grated
3 tbsp single cream
salt and freshly ground black pepper

### For the roasted greens:
200g (7oz) green beans
200g (7oz) Tenderstem broccoli
2 garlic cloves, grated
2 tbsp olive oil
150g (5½oz) Parmesan, finely grated

### YOU WILL NEED
large baking tray, roughly 38 x 27cm (15 x 10½in), lined with baking parchment
large roasting tin

1   Start with the sauce. Warm the milk in a pan over a medium heat, then add the flour and butter. Using a balloon whisk, whisk the sauce for 6 minutes, until creamy and thick. Add the garlic, turn the heat to its lowest setting and cook the sauce for a further 5 minutes, whisking every so often to ensure it doesn't catch on the bottom. Season with a little salt and pepper, to taste, then stir in the sun-dried tomato paste, Parmesan, and finally the cream. Set aside until needed.

2   Preheat the oven to 220°C (200°C fan/425°F/ Gas 7). Unroll the sheet of pastry and set aside.

3   Blanch the asparagus in a small pan of boiling water for 3 minutes, then drain and refresh in cold water. Drain again and set aside.

4   Mark out a large rectangle on the baking parchment, the same size as the pastry, and place it drawn-side down on the baking tray. Drizzle with a little olive oil, then sprinkle over the oregano and chilli flakes. Season with salt and pepper.

5   Leaving a 2cm (¾in) border, place the chicken on top of the seasoned oil, then add the asparagus. Season with more salt and pepper. Carefully pour the sauce over.

6   Drape the pastry over the top of the saucy chicken and asparagus. Using the back of a teaspoon, scallop the edges of the pastry to seal. Score the top in a diamond pattern with a sharp knife and then brush with egg.

7   Bake for 35 minutes, or until the pastry is golden and crisp. Remove the tart from the oven and allow it to sit on the tray for 5 minutes. Lay a piece of baking parchment on top, followed by a chopping board, and carefully flip the tart over. Remove the tray and peel off the backing paper. (You may want to slide the tart back onto the baking tray and into the oven for a few minutes to get a little more golden on top before serving.)

8   Meanwhile, roast the greens. Place the vegetables and garlic in a large roasting tin. Drizzle over the olive oil, add half of the Parmesan and mix well. Cook at the same time as the tart for 15–20 minutes, until tender and golden. Sprinkle the remaining Parmesan over the greens, then serve with the tart.

## Upside Down Banana & Custard Tart
### DESSERT (SERVES 2 WITH LEFTOVERS)

I asked The Viking what he would love to have for dessert if I were to make him a romantic meal, and his answer was "bananas and custard". I guess his palate is on brand with my kind of cooking: simple, homely, classic, and reminiscent of the foods we both loved in childhood. So, I made his suggestion into a tart with the golden, crisp pastry a bonus!

320g (11oz) sheet of ready-rolled puff pastry, roughly 35 x 23cm (14 x 9in), or use homemade (see p12)
drizzle of runny honey
2 bananas (slightly under-ripe is best), thickly sliced
1 egg, lightly beaten
icing sugar, for dusting
double cream, to serve

### For the custard:
175ml (6fl oz) whole milk
3 large egg yolks
20g (¾oz) golden caster sugar
1 tsp grated nutmeg, plus a little extra for sprinkling
½ tsp vanilla extract

### YOU WILL NEED
large baking tray, roughly 38 x 27cm (15 x 10½in), lined with baking parchment
22cm (8½in) diameter round plate

1   Start with the custard. Warm the milk in a pan over a medium heat until it starts to lightly simmer; do not let it boil. Remove the pan from the heat.

2   Place the egg yolks and sugar in a large bowl and whisk until pale and creamy. Slowly pour the warm milk over the egg yolks, whisking with a balloon whisk. Stir in the nutmeg and vanilla. Pour the custard mixture into a jug and set aside to cool.

3   Preheat the oven to 220°C (200°C fan/425°F/ Gas 7). Unroll the sheet of pastry. Using the 22cm (8½in) round plate as a template, cut the pastry into a disc. Place in the fridge until needed.

4   Draw around the same plate onto the baking parchment, then place it drawn-side down on the baking tray. Drizzle honey over the marked round and sprinkle with a little grated nutmeg.

5   Leaving a 2cm (¾in) border, lay the banana slices in two circles on top of the marked round (you need to create a circular ring or barrier of bananas). Now pour the custard into the middle and tuck any remaining banana slices into the custard.

6   Lay the pastry disc on top of the bananas and custard. Using the back of a teaspoon, scallop the edge of the pastry to seal. Score the top in a diamond pattern with a sharp knife and then brush with egg.

7   Bake for 30 minutes, or until the pastry is golden and crisp. Remove the tart from the oven and allow it to sit on the tray for 10 minutes. Lay a piece of baking parchment, then a chopping board or plate on top and carefully flip the tart over. Remove the tray and peel off the backing paper. Dust the top of the tart with icing sugar and serve cut into slices with cream on the side.

# Sweet
# Celebr

# ations

A feast wouldn't be a feast without a sweet conclusion, and this chapter is the ultimate in spoil-yourself treats and fun creations. From an upside-down birthday cake and twist on the traditional cream tea, through to desserts for special occasions and festivities – including Halloween, Valentine's Day, and Easter – these sweet centrepieces will take you on a celebratory journey through the year. If you're wondering why there are no Christmas recipes, for me, this festive highlight deserves its very own chapter (see pp158–81).

# Apple Tarte Tatin

The start of the year coincides with the beginning of my "upside-down" journey... perhaps I wouldn't be here today if it weren't for this classic apple tart, the origins of which really speak to me. The story revolves around the Tatin sisters, Stéphanie and Caroline, who ran the Hôtel Tatin in Lamotte-Beuvron, France. One day, Chef Stéphanie accidentally caramelized some apples for too long. To salvage the dessert, she placed a sheet of pastry on top of the fruit, then baked it, flipping the tart over to serve to guests. They loved it, and the tarte Tatin was born. This is my version, the perfect comforting dessert to brighten an often dull January.

## Serves 4

320g (11oz) sheet of ready-rolled shortcrust pastry, roughly 35 x 23cm (14 x 9in), or use homemade (see p12)

300g (10oz) golden caster sugar

1 tsp vanilla extract

100g (3½oz) salted butter, cut into cubes

8 apples (I like to use a sharp-sweet apple, like a Cox) peeled, cored, and quartered

vanilla ice cream, to serve

### YOU WILL NEED

18cm (7in) diameter heavy cast-iron, ovenproof skillet

1  Preheat the oven to 190°C (170°C fan/375°F/Gas 5). Unroll the sheet of pastry and cut a round roughly 2cm (¾in) larger than the diameter of the skillet. Place in the fridge until needed.

2  Add the sugar and vanilla to the skillet and place it on a medium heat. Let the sugar heat, without stirring, until melted and starting to form a caramel; this takes about 5 minutes. Swirl the pan until any uncooked sugar is combined with the melted sugar but do not stir it. Cook for a further 5 minutes, or until the sugar melts and has turned into a dark, golden caramel. Carefully, take the pan off the heat.

3  Dot the cubes of butter over the caramel, then carefully lay the apples in a single, even layer on top, packing them tightly into the pan. I like concentric rings of apples, but you can go freestyle here; it's up to you.

4  Once the base of the pan is covered in an even layer of apples, carefully place the pastry round on top and tuck the edges in at the sides as much as you can.

5  Bake the tarte for 30 minutes, or until the pastry is crisp and golden. Remove the tarte from the oven and allow it to stand for 10 minutes (not longer – you must turn it out while still warm or the caramel will harden and stick to the pan). Place a platter or large plate on top of the pan and carefully flip it over. Lift off the pan and serve the tarte warm, cut into slices, with a large scoop of vanilla ice cream.

# Valentine's Chocolate & Berry Lava Pie

Nothing says love like a gooey chocolate pie. This foolproof lava cake is made in a large pie dish with the addition of raspberries, which are heavenly with chocolate. It also features fennel seeds, since The Viking loves the flavour of aniseed, and they add a touch of sophistication to the dessert. It's the perfect treat for Valentine's Day.

### Serves 2 (with leftovers)

175g (6oz) salted butter
½ tsp fennel seeds (optional, but well worth it)
200g (7oz) 70% plain chocolate, chopped
3 large eggs
125g (4½oz) caster sugar
40g (1½oz) ground almonds or plain flour
200g (7oz) raspberries
cream or ice cream, to serve

### YOU WILL NEED
medium, rectangular pie dish, lightly greased with butter

1 Preheat the oven to 180°C (160°C fan/350°F/Gas 4).

2 Melt the butter with the fennel seeds, if using, in a saucepan on a medium heat. Remove from the heat and gently stir through half of the chocolate until melted.

3 In a large bowl, whisk together the eggs and sugar using an electric hand whisk until pale and fluffy. Pour in the melted chocolate mixture, then sift in the ground almonds or flour. Gently stir in the raspberries and the remaining chocolate until everything is combined. Pour the mixture into the prepared pie dish.

4 Bake for 20 minutes, until the edge of the pie is firm and darkened, and the centre is still slightly wobbly. Serve straightaway with cream or ice cream.

# Upside Down Banoffee Pie

I love a portmanteau: word games, puns, and etymology are my favourite topics of conversation, so if I come across a name of a dish that is a play on words, then I'm a happy boy. Banoffee pie is one such dish, the name is a combination of banana and toffee, which coincidentally are two of my favourite things to eat. I've included all the classic banoffee elements in this upside-down version, but in a deconstructed way. It comes with a final flourish of whipped cream.

## Serves 4–6

320g (11oz) sheet of ready-rolled puff pastry, roughly 35 x 23cm (14 x 9in), or use homemade (see p12)
50g (1¾oz) salted butter, at room temperature
4 tbsp runny honey, plus extra for drizzling
2 tbsp golden caster sugar
4 digestive biscuits
3 just-ripe bananas, peeled and thickly sliced
1 egg, lightly beaten
300ml (10fl oz) whipping or double cream
50g (1¾oz) plain chocolate, grated, to decorate

### YOU WILL NEED

large baking tray, roughly 38 x 27cm (15 x 10½in), lined with baking parchment
22cm (8½in) diameter round plate

1  Preheat the oven to 220°C (200°C fan/425°F/Gas 7). Unroll the sheet of pastry and cut out a round using the 22cm (8½in) diameter plate as a template. Place in the fridge until needed.

2  Draw around the same plate onto the baking parchment. Place the paper drawn-side down on the baking tray.

3  Spread half of the butter within the drawn circle on the baking parchment, then drizzle over half of the honey and sprinkle with half of the sugar.

4  Leaving a 1cm (½in) border, crumble two of the biscuits over the drawn circle and top with one of the sliced bananas. Repeat to create a second layer of butter, honey, sugar, biscuits, and sliced banana.

5  Drape the pastry round over the top of the banana mixture. Using the back of a fork, press around the edge of the pastry to seal. Score the top in a diamond pattern with a sharp knife and then brush with egg.

6  Bake for 30 minutes, until the pastry is golden and crisp. Remove the pie from the oven and allow it to sit on the tray for 10 minutes. Lay a piece of baking parchment on top, followed by a chopping board or plate and carefully flip it over. Remove the tray and peel off the backing paper, then leave the pie to cool.

7  Meanwhile, whip the cream to medium-soft peaks. Spoon the cream over the cooled tart and top with the remaining sliced banana, the grated chocolate, and an extra drizzle of honey.

# Upside Down Carrot Cake

If I'm in a cafe or bakery, I almost always order carrot cake and I also love to make it at home. This is my go-to recipe, inspired by Delia Smith's ultimate carrot cake, which I've been baking, adapting, and enjoying for decades. It's the perfect cake for any Easter celebrations you're planning.

## Serves 8

### For the cake:
175g (6oz) soft dark brown sugar
2 large eggs
150ml (5fl oz) sunflower oil
150g (5½oz) self-raising flour
50g (1¾oz) ground almonds
1 tsp ground ginger
1 tsp ground cinnamon
1 tsp bicarbonate of soda
200g (7oz) carrots, peeled
    and finely grated
grated zest of 1 orange
110g (3¾oz) mixed dried fruit
    and candied peel
50g (1¾oz) desiccated coconut

### For the topping:
50g (1oz) caster sugar
6 long, slim, heritage carrots,
    halved lengthways
small knob of salted butter
2 tbsp runny honey, plus extra
    to serve

### For the cinnamon cream:
150ml (5fl oz) whipping or
    double cream
100g (3½oz) cream cheese
1 tbsp icing sugar
1 tsp ground cinnamon
finely grated zest of 1 orange

### YOU WILL NEED
20cm (8in) round cake tin,
    lined with baking parchment

1  Preheat the oven to 190°C (170°C fan/375°F/Gas 5).

2  To make the topping, bring a pan of boiling water to the boil, stir in the sugar and add the carrots. Return the water to the boil, then turn the heat down to low and simmer for 10 minutes, or until the carrots are just tender. Drain well.

3  Spread a little butter over the lined base of the cake tin and drizzle with 1 tablespoon of the honey. Arrange the cooked carrots in the tin, cut-side down. Trim the carrots, if needed, so they fit tightly and neatly, then drizzle with the remaining honey.

4  To make the cake, whisk the sugar, eggs, and oil in a large bowl for 2–3 minutes using an electric hand whisk until smooth and creamy (a stand mixer would also work well here). Sift the flour, almonds, spices, and bicarbonate of soda into the bowl, then whisk on a low speed until evenly combined. Fold in the rest of the cake ingredients and tip the mixture into the prepared cake tin on top of the candied carrots. Smooth the top with a palette knife.

5  Bake for 45 minutes, until the cake is golden and risen, and a skewer inserted into the middle comes out clean. Remove from the oven and leave the cake to cool in the tin on a wire rack.

6  Meanwhile, make the cinnamon cream. Whisk the cream to soft peaks in a large bowl, then add the cream cheese, icing sugar, cinnamon, and orange zest and whisk again to firm peaks. Place in the fridge until needed.

7  Turn the cake out of the tin onto a serving plate or cake stand and remove the backing paper. Serve cut into slices with a large spoonful of the cinnamon cream. Finish with an extra drizzle of honey.

# Pear & Pistachio Crinkle Cake

I love spring. The longer days, brighter skies, and the promise of summer around the corner, which really helps, as I have occasional bouts of anxiety during the darker, colder months. At times like this, I find baking incredibly therapeutic. A calming distraction. This cake is perfect for that – the folding of the pastry, the sprinkling of the nuts, and preparation of the fruit – plus, you're rewarded with a delicious bake at the end.

## Serves 8

### For the cake:

150g (5½oz) shelled, unsalted pistachios, plus extra to decorate

250g (9oz) pack of filo pastry (you need 10 sheets)

roughly 150g (5½oz) salted butter, melted, plus extra for greasing

5 tbsp caster sugar, plus extra for sprinkling

2 just-ripe pears, halved lengthways, core removed, and thinly sliced (no need to peel)

honey and Greek yogurt, to serve

### For the custard:

250ml (9fl oz) whole milk

½ tsp vanilla extract

250ml (9fl oz) single cream

3 large eggs

1 large egg yolk

2 tbsp caster sugar

1 tbsp almond butter (or other nut butter or chocolate hazelnut spread)

### YOU WILL NEED

22cm (8½in) round ovenproof dish, such as a flan dish or similar, greased

1   To make the custard, place the milk, vanilla, and single cream in a small saucepan and gently heat to a simmer. Take the pan off the heat and allow the mixture to cool. You want it to be barely warm.

2   Crack the eggs into a large bowl. Add the extra yolk, sugar, and almond butter, and whisk with an electric hand whisk. Once combined, gradually pour in the warm milk in a steady stream, continuing to whisk on a low speed. Set aside once all the milk has been added.

3   Using the end of a rolling pin, or mini food processor in pulse mode, crush the pistachios to a rough crumble. Set aside.

4   Lay a sheet of filo pastry on your work surface and brush it with a little melted butter (this doesn't have to be perfectly done), then sprinkle with roughly 1 tablespoon of the crushed pistachios and ½ tablespoon of caster sugar. Pleat the sheet of filo like a fan into a 4cm (1½in) wide strip, or the same width as the depth of your dish, enclosing the pistachios and sugar within the folds. Place the strip of folded filo around the inside edge of the dish. Repeat with the remaining sheets of filo, pistachios, and sugar, arranging the strips in the dish in a circle, working from the outside inwards in a fairly tight spiral, and slightly overlapping the edge of each pastry strip. Continue until you've used all the pastry sheets.

5   Preheat the oven to 190°C (170°C fan/375°F/Gas 5). Carefully press slices of pear between the folds of the filo pastry. Pour the custard over the top and sprinkle with extra sugar. Bake for 45 minutes, or until the top of the cake is golden and risen, and the custard has set.

6   To finish, drizzle the top with honey and sprinkle with extra crushed pistachios. Serve cut into slices with Greek yogurt.

# Upside Down School Cake Tart

Kids of every generation love this cake (it was my favourite part of school dinners). The classic vanilla traybake is topped with a simple icing and decorated with a sprinkling of hundreds and thousands. It's usually served cut into squares with lashings of vanilla custard, but this version comes with an upside-down twist.

**Serves 12**

**For the tart:**

320g (11oz) sheet of ready-rolled puff pastry, roughly 35 x 23cm (14 x 9in), or use homemade (see p12)
2 tbsp seedless strawberry jam
drizzle of runny honey
2 tbsp hundreds and thousands multi-coloured sprinkles

**For the cake:**

140g (5oz) salted butter, softened, plus extra for greasing
140g (5oz) caster sugar
2 large eggs, lightly beaten
140g (5oz) self-raising flour, sifted
1 tsp vanilla extract

**For the icing:**

200g (7oz) icing sugar, sifted
hundreds and thousands multi-coloured sprinkles, to decorate
hot custard, to serve

**YOU WILL NEED**

large baking tray, roughly 38 x 27cm (15 x 10½in), lined with baking parchment

1 Preheat the oven to 200°C (180°C fan/400°F/Gas 6). Unroll the sheet of pastry and spread a thin layer of jam over one side, leaving a 2cm (¾in) border. Place in the fridge until needed.

2 Mark out a large rectangle, the same size as the pastry, on the baking parchment and place it drawn-side down on the baking tray. Drizzle the lined baking tray with honey and sprinkle with the hundreds and thousands. Set aside.

3 To make the cake, cream the butter and sugar in a large bowl using an electric hand whisk until pale and fluffy. Add the eggs, flour, and vanilla and beat again to a smooth, thick cake batter. Pour the batter onto the lined baking tray and spread it out evenly over the marked rectangle, leaving a 1cm (½in) border. It should be fairly thick and not run too much.

4 Carefully drape the pastry, jam-side down, over the cake batter. Using a teaspoon, scallop the edges of the pastry to seal. Score the top in a diamond pattern with a sharp knife and then brush with egg.

5 Bake for 35 minutes, or until the pastry is golden, and the cake is risen and cooked. Remove the tart from the oven and allow it to rest on the tray for 10 minutes. Lay a piece of baking parchment on top, followed by a chopping board, and carefully flip it over. Remove the tray and peel off the backing paper, then leave to cool.

6 To decorate the tart, mix the icing sugar with enough water to make a thick icing. Spread the icing over the cooled cake, then decorate the top generously with sprinkles. Leave for about 1 hour, until the icing has set, then cut into squares and serve with hot custard.

# Cream Tea Cobbler

This takes the elements of a classic English cream tea – scone, strawberry jam, and thick clotted cream – and transforms them into a treat of a dessert. And you don't even have to worry about whether to top your scone with cream or jam first as everything is smooshed together in one delightful dish!

## Serves 6

300g (10oz) self-raising flour
100g (3½oz) cold lightly salted butter, cut into small cubes
100g (3½oz) caster sugar
1 egg, lightly beaten
4 tbsp whole milk or buttermilk
400g (14oz) strawberries, hulled, cut in half, if large, others left whole
225g (8oz) clotted cream
extra clotted cream or ice cream, to serve

**YOU WILL NEED**
20cm (8in) round ovenproof dish, base and sides greased

1 Preheat the oven to 200°C (180°C fan/400°F/Gas 6). Using your fingertips, rub the flour and butter together in a large bowl to a breadcrumb consistency. Add the sugar, egg, and milk or buttermilk and, using a butter knife, bring everything together into a loose, shaggy dough.

2 Tip half of the strawberries into the ovenproof dish, followed by a few dollops of the clotted cream (about half). Add half of the cobbler dough on top of the strawberries in large spoonfuls. Repeat with the remaining strawberries, cream, and the cobbler dough. You don't have to be neat when assembling this dish – it should all be quite random.

3 Bake for 35–40 minutes, until the cobbler topping has risen and become golden. Remove from the oven and leave to cool slightly. Serve the cobbler with extra clotted cream or ice cream.

# Plum & Chilli Jam Galette

Plums, particularly Victoria, are my absolute favourite end-of-summer fruit. They remind me of my childhood: picking plums in the back garden at home, avoiding wasps, and getting belly ache from eating far too many. They cook beautifully, releasing so much juice and flavour, which is enhanced here by the spicy chilli jam. This simple but elegant galette is the perfect way to celebrate the arrival of late summer fruit.

## Serves 6

### For the pastry:
150g (5½oz) wholemeal flour
150g (5½oz) plain flour, plus
    extra for dusting
200g (7oz) cold salted
    butter, cubed
1 tbsp golden caster sugar
splash of ice-cold water
1 egg, lightly beaten

### For the filling:
roughly 10 plums (I like
    Victoria)
1 tbsp golden caster sugar,
    plus extra for sprinkling
juice and finely grated zest
    of 1 lemon
2 tbsp apricot jam
good pinch of chilli flakes
handful of flaked almonds

### YOU WILL NEED
large baking tray, roughly
    38 x 27cm (15 x 10½in),
    greased and lined with
    baking parchment

1   To make the pastry, place both types of flour and the butter into a large bowl and rub together with your fingertips until the mixture resembles breadcrumbs. Stir in the sugar, then add a splash or two of ice-cold water. Using one hand, shaped like a claw, mix everything together into a ball of dough, adding more water if needed. Flatten the dough into a disc, then wrap it in cling film and chill for 30 minutes.

2   While the pastry is chilling, halve and destone the plums, then cut them into slices. Place the plums in a bowl, then stir in the sugar and lemon juice and zest.

3   Preheat the oven to 180°C (160°C fan/350°F/Gas 4).

4   Generously dust your work surface with flour and roll out the pastry to roughly the same size as the lined baking tray. I like an oval shape, but this is a rustic tart so don't worry too much about uniformity. Carefully lift the pastry onto the tray.

5   Spread the jam evenly over the pastry, then scatter over the chilli flakes and top with the plums (you can go for uniform rows or just pile them on, it's totally up to you), leaving a 5cm (2in) border around the edge. Fold the edge of the pastry over the plum filling, gathering it where needed to make an open-topped oval tart.

6   Brush the edges of the pastry with egg, then sprinkle with flaked almonds and a little sugar. Bake for 35–45 minutes, until the pastry is golden and crisp, and the plums have softened. Leave to cool for 5 minutes or so on the tray, then serve cut into slices.

# Upside Down Crumble Tart

It just so happens that The Viking and I share the same birthday. On the surface, this sounds like a joyous thing, a double celebration, fun for all, but no, he is not a birthday fan. I have tried to make him fall in love with "our" day, and over the years, I think I've softened him to enjoy it more, and I've done this through food. This year, I asked him what his favourite type of birthday cake would be, and he said "peach or nectarine crumble". So, here it is in tart form...

**Serves 6**

**For the pastry:**
320g (11oz) sheet of ready-
    rolled puff pastry, roughly
    35 x 23cm (14 x 9in), or use
    homemade (see p12)
2 tbsp chocolate spread
drizzle of runny honey
2 tbsp caster sugar
1 egg, lightly beaten

**For the crumble:**
50g (1¾oz) plain flour
30g (1oz) rolled oats
50g (1¾oz) caster sugar
50g (1¾oz) cold butter, cubed

**For the cake:**
60g (2oz) self-raising flour
60g (2oz) salted butter,
    softened, cut into cubes
60g (2oz) caster sugar
1 large egg
splash of whole milk
½ tsp vanilla extract
1 large ripe peach or nectarine,
    stone removed and
    flesh chopped

**YOU WILL NEED**
large baking tray, roughly
    38 x 27cm (15 x 10½in),
    lined with baking parchment
22cm (8½in) diameter
    round plate

1   Preheat the oven to 220°C (200°C fan/425°F/Gas 7). Unroll the sheet of pastry and cut out a 22cm (8½in) round using the plate as a template. Spread the chocolate spread over one side of the pastry and fold it in half. Gently roll the pastry out again into a round slightly larger than the 22cm (8½in) round plate. Place in the fridge until needed.

2   Draw around the plate onto the baking parchment and place the paper drawn-side down on the baking tray. Drizzle over a little honey and sprinkle with the sugar.

3   To make the crumble, using your fingertips, rub all the ingredients together in a bowl until they come together in large clumps – you don't want the mixture to be too fine. Set aside.

4   Whisk all the cake ingredients (apart from the fruit) in a large bowl using an electric hand whisk until light and creamy. This should take roughly 5 minutes.

5   With a spoon, dot some of the crumble mix randomly over the drawn circle on the lined baking tray, then add a few spoonfuls of the cake batter and a scattering of peach or nectarine. Continue to build the cake in layers of crumble, cake batter, and fruit, then use your hands to gently press the mixture into a rough dome shape as you build.

6   Lay the pastry over the pile of crumble, cake, and fruit. Using the back of a teaspoon, scallop the edge to seal. Score the top in a diamond pattern with a sharp knife and then brush with egg.

7   Bake for 30 minutes, or until the pastry is golden and the cake is risen and firm. Remove the tart from the oven and allow it to sit on a wire rack for 5 minutes. Lay a piece of baking parchment and a chopping board or cake stand on top and flip it over. Remove the tray and peel off the backing paper to reveal the tart. Serve cut into slices.

# Spider's Web Upside Down Fruit Tart

Halloween is such a fun festival for kids and adults alike. While I adore Christmas treats, you can get away with being more creative at Halloween, combining spooky with tasty in one dish. This tart has both – the wow factor with its spidery decoration and blood-red berry and apple filling, and it also tastes fantastic.

## Serves 6–8

2 x 320g (11oz) sheets of ready-rolled puff pastry, roughly 35 x 23cm (14 x 9in), or use homemade (see p12)
75g (2½oz) salted butter, softened
1 tbsp golden caster sugar
2 cooking apples, peeled, cored, and cut into small cubes
3 tbsp mixed frozen berries
1 egg, lightly beaten

### For the spider:
2 tbsp lemon curd
2 frozen blueberries for eyes

### YOU WILL NEED
2 large baking trays, roughly 38 x 27cm (15 x 10½in), lined with baking parchment
10cm (4in) fluted cookie cutter
piping bag with small nozzle

1 Preheat the oven to 220°C (200°C fan/425°F/Gas 7). Unroll one of the sheets of pastry, placing it vertically in front of you. Cut the pastry into 1cm (½in) wide strips, then place them on a tray in the fridge until needed.

2 Smear the butter all over the lined baking tray and sprinkle with the sugar. Arrange the pastry strips in a spider's web pattern on the lined tray (see pic, left).

3 Place the apples in a bowl and mix in the berries, then gently tip the mixture on top of the pastry spider's web in a rough rectangular heap in the middle, leaving a 2cm (¾in) border.

4 Unroll the second sheet of pastry, cut off a 10cm (4in) wide strip from one of short ends to make the spider, then set aside in the fridge. Drape the larger piece of pastry over the apple mixture and trim the edges to neaten. Using the back of a fork, press around the edge of the pastry to seal. Score the top in a diamond pattern with a sharp knife and then brush with egg, leaving some to glaze the spider.

5 Bake for 30–35 minutes, until the pastry is golden and crisp. Remove the tart from the oven and allow it to sit on the tray for 5 minutes. Lay a piece of baking parchment on top, followed by a chopping board, and carefully flip the tart over. Remove the tray and lift off the backing paper.

6 While the tart is baking, make the spider. Using the cookie cutter, stamp out a disc of puff pastry for the body and cut 8 thin strips for the legs. Twist and bend the pastry legs and place on a second lined baking tray with the spider's body. Brush with egg and bake for about 15 minutes, or until golden and puffed up. Leave to cool on a wire rack. Spoon the lemon curd into the piping bag. Make a hole in the side of the spider's body, insert the piping bag and squeeze in the curd. Carefully make four holes down each side of the body and insert the legs. Pipe small blobs of the lemon curd to make two eyes and top with the berries. Place the spider on top of the tart to serve.

# Pumpkin Upside Down Pie

When I reached the sixth form (the last two years of senior school), the boys in my year started to mix socially with girls from the school across the road, for obvious reasons. Clearly, those reasons didn't interest me, but to finally have some girl friends was heaven. This is when I met Shannon, who is still my friend today. Her family was American, and they introduced me to pumpkin pie. This is my tribute to her.

## Serves 6

320g (11oz) sheet of ready-rolled puff pastry, roughly 35 x 23cm (14 x 9in), or use homemade (see p12)
320g (11oz) sheet of ready-rolled shortcrust pastry, roughly 35 x 23cm (14 x 9in), or use homemade (see p12)
sprinkle each of ground cinnamon and caster sugar
drizzle of runny honey
1 tbsp demerara sugar
1 egg, lightly beaten

### For the pie filling:
3 eggs
175g (6oz) caster sugar
1 tsp mixed spice
200g (7oz) canned pumpkin purée
100ml (3½fl oz) double cream
1 tsp ground cinnamon
½ tsp ground ginger
double cream, to serve

### YOU WILL NEED
large baking tray, roughly 38 x 27cm (15 x 10½in), lined with baking parchment
20cm (8in) diameter round plate
leaf-shaped pastry cutters

1  Preheat the oven to 200°C (180°C fan/400°F/Gas 6). Unroll both sheets of pastry. Cut out a 20cm (8in) round of puff pastry using the plate as a template. Sprinkle a light dusting of cinnamon and caster sugar over the puff pastry round and the shortcrust sheet. Put the puff pastry in the fridge until needed. Using the leaf-shaped cutters or a sharp knife, cut out as many leaves as possible using the shortcrust pastry – I like to use two different sizes of leaf. Place them on a tray in the fridge.

2  To make the pie filling, beat the eggs and caster sugar in a large bowl with an electric hand whisk until light and fluffy. Whisk in half of the mixed spice with the rest of the filling ingredients until combined. Set aside.

3  Draw around the plate onto the baking parchment and place the paper drawn-side down on the baking tray. Drizzle over a little honey, then sprinkle with the remaining mixed spice and the demerara sugar. Brush a thick line of beaten egg around the marked line and arrange the pastry leaves on top. I like to place the leaves in a random pattern, overlapping them to form a circular wreath border. Repeat to make a double layer of leaves, and a barrier to hold in the pie filling. Brush the leaves with some of the beaten egg.

4  Pour in the pie filling, then drape the disc of puff pastry over the top. Using the back of a fork, press around the edge of the pastry to seal it to the decorative leaf border. Score the top in a diamond pattern with a sharp knife and then brush with egg.

5  Bake for 35–40 minutes, until the pastry is golden and crisp. Remove the pie from the oven and allow it to sit for at least 1 hour to cool and set. Lay a piece of baking parchment on top, followed by a chopping board or serving platter, and carefully flip it over. Remove the tray and peel off the backing paper. Serve the pie cut into slices with double cream.

# chris time

# **mas-**

For a nice Jewish boy from north London, Christmas holds a special place in my heart. I guess it's because we didn't really celebrate it when I was a kid. Don't get me wrong, Father Christmas always came, and we would often visit relatives for the big-day meal, but we never put up a tree or decorations. It was just one day, then over. Now I'm grown up, with my own home, we go big. The first day of December is the start for us. A real tree goes up, there are decorations everywhere, and the feasting begins. After all, I need little excuse to celebrate. And it's not just Christmas Day. There are myriad occasions to feast: from impromptu December parties to Boxing Day get-togethers, and beyond to New Year's Eve. This chapter is a collection of festive meals and party treats to cater for everyone, from large gatherings to more intimate soirées.

# Caramelized Onion, Stuffing & Veggie Roast Christmas Pudding

The Viking says the worst thing about being a vegetarian is Christmas lunch. He's happy with just the vegetables and all the trimmings, but if I really want to go to town, I make this beauty, inspired by a recipe by the great Nigel Slater a few years ago. It's a savoury pudding that takes the flavours of Christmas and layers them in a vegetable suet pastry case with delicious results. Serve it with your favourite Christmas sides and trimmings – and veggie gravy, of course!

## Serves 6

### For the filling:
50g (1¾oz) butter
1 tbsp olive oil
4 large onions, finely sliced
1 tsp chopped rosemary leaves
1 tsp thyme leaves
200g (7oz) vegetarian roast, such as Quorn (or similar favourite meat-free protein)
175g (6oz) packet of sage and onion stuffing
salt and freshly ground black pepper

### For the suet pastry:
300g (10oz) self-raising flour, plus extra for dusting
150g (5½oz) vegetarian suet
1 tsp chopped rosemary leaves
1 tsp chopped thyme leaves
200ml (7fl oz) ice-cold water

### YOU WILL NEED
(900g) 2lb pudding basin, greased generously with butter

1  First, caramelize the onions. Heat the butter and olive oil in a large frying pan on a medium heat. Add the onions and cook gently for 30 minutes, stirring every 10 minutes or so (you may need to turn the heat down slightly to prevent them burning and sticking to the bottom of the pan), until caramelized. Add the herbs and cook for a further minute, stirring occasionally. Season with salt and pepper to taste, then set aside to cool.

2  Meanwhile, cook the vegetarian roast according to the packet instructions, then cut it into roughly 12 thick slices. Make the stuffing mix following the packet instructions. Set aside.

3  To make the suet pastry, in a large bowl, mix the flour, suet, herbs, water, and a pinch of salt together to form a soft ball of dough. On a lightly floured work surface, roll out the dough until roughly 5mm (¼in) thick. Set aside enough pastry to make the lid, using the top of the bowl as a template, then use the remaining pastry to line the well-greased pudding basin.

4  Begin to assemble the pudding, alternating between layers of caramelized onions, slices of veggie roast (you may need to trim them), and stuffing until the filling almost reaches the top of the pudding basin. Brush the edge of the pastry with water, then place the pastry lid on top and press the edges together to seal.

5  Cover the top of the basin with a round of baking parchment and then foil, making a pleat down the middle of both to allow the pudding to expand, then secure with string. Place the basin in a steamer and cook for 1 hour, topping up with more water, if needed. (Alternatively, place on an inverted bowl in a saucepan with enough water to come halfway up the sides of the basin.)

6  Carefully remove the basin from the pan and let it sit for 10 minutes, then remove the foil and paper. Slice the pudding into wedges and serve with the Christmas trimmings.

# Upside Down Sausage, Brie & Cranberry Tart

If you're looking for an alternative to roast turkey, this tart makes a wonderful, all-in-one option for the big day. Combining classic festive ingredients, this simple recipe can be adapted to suit different tastes by adding your favourite herbs, spices, and other flavourings to the sausagemeat. This version, however, is a good starting point and comes with my upside-down twist. It's one the whole family will love!

## Serves 4–6

320g (11oz) sheet of ready-rolled puff pastry, roughly 35 x 23cm (14 x 9in), or use homemade (see p12)
175g (6oz) packet of stuffing mix (I like sage and onion)
drizzle of olive oil
1 tsp chopped rosemary leaves, plus extra to garnish
1 tsp chopped thyme leaves
150g (5½oz) sausagemeat
100g (3½oz) Brie, cut into thick slices
2 tbsp cranberry sauce
1 egg, lightly beaten
salt and freshly ground black pepper

### YOU WILL NEED

large baking tray, roughly 38 x 27cm (15 x 10½in), lined with baking parchment

1   Preheat the oven to 220°C (200°C fan/425°F/Gas 7). Unroll the sheet of pastry and set aside.

2   Make the stuffing mix according to the instructions on the packet – I like to add a drizzle of olive oil to mine. Leave to cool.

3   Leaving a 1cm (½in) border, spread the stuffing mix over the pastry, then place in the fridge until needed.

4   Mark out a large rectangle on the baking paper, the same size as the pastry, and place it drawn-side down on the baking tray. Drizzle olive oil over the lined baking tray, then sprinkle with the rosemary and thyme. Season with salt and pepper.

5   Leaving a 2cm (¾in) border, press the sausagemeat in an even layer over the drawn rectangle. Lay the slices of Brie on top of the sausagemeat and dot spoonfuls of the cranberry sauce over.

6   Carefully drape the pastry sheet, stuffing-side down, over the Brie and sausagemeat mixture. Using the back of a teaspoon, scallop the edges of the pastry to seal. Score the top in a diamond pattern with a sharp knife and then brush with egg.

7   Bake for 30–35 minutes, until the pastry is golden and crisp. Remove the tart from the oven and allow it to sit on the tray for 5 minutes. Lay a piece of baking parchment on top, followed by a chopping board, then flip the tart over. Remove the tray and peel off the backing paper to serve.

# Upside Down Camembert & Chilli Jam Snowflake

Is there anything more decadent and luscious than hot, melted Camembert baked in a golden puff pastry case? The combination screams Christmas to me, and this tear-and-share treat is perfect for festive parties or as a starter on the big day itself.

**Serves 4–6**

2 x 320g (11oz) sheets of ready-rolled puff pastry, roughly 35 x 23cm (14 x 9in), or use homemade (see p12)
3 tbsp chilli jam (or mix half-and-half with Red Onion Jam, see p15)
drizzle of olive oil
1 tsp thyme leaves
250g (9oz) whole Camembert, packaging removed
1 egg, lightly beaten
salt and freshly ground black pepper

**YOU WILL NEED**
large baking tray, roughly 38 x 27cm (15 x 10½in), lined with baking parchment
22cm (8½in) diameter round plate

1 Preheat the oven to 220°C (200°C fan/425°F/Gas 7). Unroll both sheets of pastry and cut out 2 large rounds using the 22cm (8½in) plate as a template. Using a rolling pin, roll out the pastry rounds to make them 2cm (¾in) larger in diameter. Spread the chilli jam over one side of one of the pastry rounds and lay the second round of pastry on top. Place in the fridge until needed.

2 Drizzle olive oil over the lined baking tray and sprinkle with the thyme. Season with salt and pepper. Place the Camembert in the middle of the tray and drape the pastry sandwich over the top. Press the sides of the pastry down to encase the cheese and form a pastry "skirt".

3 Make 12 evenly spaced cuts around the pastry "skirt", each one running from the cheese to the edge of the pastry. Take 2 strips of the pastry and twist them together, pressing the ends together in a point. Continue with the remaining strips of pastry to form six points. Score the top of the pastry in a diamond pattern with a sharp knife and then brush with egg.

4 Bake for 30–35 minutes, until the pastry is golden and crisp. Remove the pastry snowflake from the oven and allow it to sit on the tray for 5 minutes. Lay a piece of baking parchment on top, followed by a chopping board, then flip the whole thing over. Remove the tray and peel off the backing paper.

5 To serve, make a hole in the middle of the Camembert, then break off the points of the snowflake to dunk into the melted cheese filling.

# Upside Down Parsnip, Honey & Thyme Tarts

If you're anything like me, parsnips rarely get a look-in outside of the Christmas lunch (apart from a spicy parsnip soup, perhaps, which I only make if I've bought too many parsnips for Christmas). I know the vegetable can be divisive, but I can assure you, this slightly sweet and fragrant tart, with a sharp hit from the grainy mustard, will make you question why you don't eat parsnips more often. This tart makes a great side dish or a vegetarian main course.

**Serves 2–4**

320g (11oz) sheet of ready-rolled puff pastry, roughly 35 x 23cm (14 x 9in), or use homemade (see p12)
2 tbsp wholegrain mustard
drizzle of olive oil
1 tsp thyme leaves, plus extra to garnish
2 tbsp runny honey
4 parsnips, peeled, trimmed, and halved lengthways
100g (3½oz) Gruyère, grated
1 egg, lightly beaten
salt and freshly ground black pepper

**YOU WILL NEED**
large baking tray, roughly 38 x 27cm (15 x 10½in), lined with baking parchment

1  Preheat the oven to 220°C (200°C fan/425°F/Gas 7). Unroll the sheet of pastry and cut it into 2 rectangles, each about 17 x 23cm (6½ x 9in). Spread 1 tablespoon of the mustard over each rectangle, leaving a narrow border. Place in the fridge until needed.

2  Mark out 2 rectangles on the baking parchment, the same size as the pastry and with space between each one, and place drawn-side down on the baking tray. Drizzle olive oil over the lined baking tray and sprinkle with the thyme. Season with salt and pepper, then drizzle over the honey.

3  Leaving a 2cm (¾in) border, arrange the parsnips on top of each drawn rectangle – I use 4 parsnip halves per tart, placed cut-side down. Scatter the Gruyère over the parsnips.

4  Drape a pastry rectangle, mustard-side down, over each pile of parsnips. Using the back of a teaspoon, scallop the edges of each tart to seal. Score the tops in a diamond pattern with a sharp knife and then brush with egg.

5  Bake for 30–35 minutes, until the pastry is golden and crisp. Remove the tarts from the oven and allow them to sit on the tray for 5 minutes. Lay a piece of baking parchment on top, followed by a chopping board, and carefully flip the tarts over. Remove the tray and peel off the backing paper. Serve warm sprinkled with thyme.

# Upside Down Brussels Sprout & Prosciutto Puffs

If you need to produce canapés at a moment's notice during the festive period, these little beauties use store cupboard ingredients and the humble, and much maligned, Brussels sprout, turning them into well-dressed puffs of festive joy.

## Makes 12

320g (11oz) sheet of ready-
    rolled puff pastry, roughly
    35 x 23cm (14 x 9in), or use
    homemade (see p12)
6 tsp cranberry sauce or jelly
drizzle of olive oil
drizzle of balsamic vinegar
100g (3½oz) Parmesan,
    finely grated
6 Brussels sprouts, halved
    lengthways
4 slices of prosciutto, each
    slice cut into 3 pieces
1 egg, lightly beaten
salt and freshly ground
    black pepper

### YOU WILL NEED
large baking tray, roughly
    38 x 27cm (15 x 10½in),
    lined with baking parchment
7cm (2¾in) plain cookie cutter
    or ramekin

1   Preheat the oven to 220°C (200°C fan/425°F/Gas 7). Unroll the sheet of pastry and, using the cookie cutter, stamp out 12 rounds. Spread ½ teaspoon of cranberry sauce in the middle of each round, leaving a narrow border. Place them on a tray in the fridge until needed.

2   Using the same cookie cutter as a template, draw 12 rounds (4 rounds across and 3 deep) evenly spaced apart on the sheet of baking parchment. Place the paper drawn-side down on the baking tray. Drizzle olive oil over the lined baking tray and add a few splashes of balsamic vinegar. Season with salt and pepper.

3   Sprinkle the Parmesan evenly over the drawn rounds. Place half a sprout, cut-side down, in the middle of each one and lay a piece of prosciutto on top.

4   Place the pastry rounds, cranberry sauce-side down, over each sprout. Using the back of a teaspoon, scallop the edges of each one to seal. Score a cross on top of the puffs with a sharp knife and then brush with egg.

5   Bake for 25 minutes, until the pastry is golden and crisp. Remove the puffs from the oven and allow them to sit on the tray for 5 minutes, then slide a palette knife under each one to flip over before serving.

# Upside Down Christmas Leftovers Quiche

In my first book, *"Upside Down Cooking"*, I created the Leftover Christmas Pie, which was a delicious way of using up any surplus roast turkey, veg, and stuffing left over from lunch. Well, here's its worthy successor... this tart has since become legendary in our home.

**Serves 4–6**

320g (11oz) sheet of ready-rolled puff pastry, roughly 35 x 23cm (14 x 9in), or use homemade (see p12)
about 400g (14oz) mix of Christmas leftovers, including turkey, pigs in blankets, roast potatoes, mashed potatoes, and stuffing, roughly chopped
3 eggs, lightly beaten
1 tbsp double cream
50g (1¾oz) feta
50g (1¾oz) Cheddar, finely grated
drizzle of olive oil
salt and freshly ground black pepper
gravy, for dunking (optional)

**YOU WILL NEED**
large baking tray, roughly 38 x 27cm (15 x 10½in), lined with baking parchment

1   Preheat the oven to 220°C (200°C fan/425°F/Gas 7). Unroll the sheet of pastry and set it aside.

2   Tip the Christmas leftovers into a large bowl and pour over the beaten egg and cream. Add the feta and Cheddar and stir well – the mixture should start to come together into a rough ball.

3   Mark out a large rectangle on the baking paper, the same size as the pastry, and place it drawn-side down on the baking tray. Drizzle over a little olive oil and season with salt and pepper.

4   Leaving a 2cm (¾in) border, spoon the Christmas quiche mixture on top of the drawn rectangle in an even layer.

5   Carefully drape the pastry over the quiche mixture. Using the back of a fork, press down the edges of the pastry to seal. Score the top in a diamond pattern with a sharp knife and then brush with egg.

6   Bake for 25–35 minutes, until the pastry is golden and crisp. Remove the tart from the oven and allow it to sit on the tray for 5 minutes. Place a piece of baking parchment on top, followed by a chopping board, and flip the tart over. Remove the tray and peel off the backing paper. Serve the slices of quiche with a pot of gravy for dunking.

# Upside Down Mince Pie

This pie has become my go-to alternative to individual mince pies. You can make your own mincemeat but I always use shop-bought, then add flavourings, such as orange and sometimes brandy. However, I always make my extra-special Christmas cream cheese and almond pastry. It's the best!

**Serves 12**

**For the pastry:**

300g (10oz) plain flour, plus
    extra for dusting
¾ tsp baking powder
110g (3¾oz) caster sugar
150g (5½oz) cold unsalted
    butter, cut into small cubes
150g (5½oz) full-fat cream
    cheese
75g (2½oz) ground almonds
1 egg yolk
splash of whole milk (optional)

**For the rest of the tart:**

75g (2½oz) unsalted butter,
    softened
1 tbsp runny honey
finely grated zest of 1 orange
400g (14oz) shop-bought
    mincemeat
1 egg, lightly beaten
icing sugar, for dusting
brandy butter or cream, to serve

**YOU WILL NEED**

large baking tray, roughly
    38 x 27cm (15 x 10½in),
    lined with baking parchment

1   To make the pastry, sift the flour, baking powder, and sugar into a large bowl. Using your fingertips, rub the butter into the dry ingredients until the mixture resembles breadcrumbs. Add the cream cheese, ground almonds, and egg yolk. Using the flat blade of a dinner knife, mix everything together to make a dough – you may need to add a little milk to help it bind. Shape the dough into a ball, wrap in cling film, and chill for at least 30 minutes. (The pastry can be made up to 24 hours in advance and kept in the fridge or frozen for 3 months.)

2   Dust the worktop with plenty of flour. (The pastry is very short and crumbly, so be generous with the flour and gentle when you roll, plus flour will help when weaving the pastry lattice.) Cut the pastry in half and then roll out each half into a 40 x 25cm (16 x 10in) rectangle. Place one half in the fridge until needed. Take the other rectangle and cut lengthways into 2cm (¾in) wide strips. Set aside.

3   Preheat the oven to 220°C (200°C fan/425°F/Gas 7). To assemble the tart, smear the softened butter over the lined baking tray. Drizzle over the honey and sprinkle with the orange zest.

4   Lay half of the pastry strips diagonally on the baking tray, placing them about 2.5cm (1in) apart. Now weave the remaining pastry strips over and under the strips on the baking tray, arranging them in a criss-cross pattern so it looks like a woven basket. Alternatively, for an easier option, place the remaining strips diagonally on top. Carefully spoon the mincemeat over.

5   Drape the remaining pastry rectangle over the mincemeat and trim the edges of the pie to neaten. Using the back of a spoon, scallop the edges of the pastry to seal. Score the top in a diamond pattern with a sharp knife and then brush with egg.

6   Bake for 30–35 minutes, until the pastry is golden and crisp. Remove the pie from the oven and allow it to sit on the tray for 5 minutes. Lay a piece of baking parchment on top, followed by a chopping board, and carefully flip the pie over. Remove the board and peel off the backing paper. Allow to cool slightly, then dust with icing sugar. Serve with brandy butter or cream.

# Upside Down Clementine & Almond Cake

Every Christmas, I like to make a clementine cake based on one by the fabulous Nigella Lawson (the origins of which are attributed to the revered Claudia Roden and her classic orange and almond cake). It's always hugely popular, and it turns out that many people across the world have their own version of this cake too, some including chocolate or made with other citrus fruits. Here, I've given the cake my upside-down twist by adding a layer of orange-infused crumble at the bottom (which becomes the top when turned over), adding a wonderful crunchy dimension to the bake.

**Serves 8**

**For the cake:**
roughly 375g (13oz)
   clementines, oranges, or
   other citrus fruit
6 large eggs, lightly beaten
225g (8oz) granulated sugar
250g (9oz) ground almonds
1 tsp baking powder

**For the crumble:**
100g (3½oz) caster sugar
50g (1¾oz) demerara sugar
finely grated zest of
   2 large oranges
150g (5½oz) cold lightly salted
   butter, cut into small cubes
100g (3½oz) muesli or
   porridge oats
150g (5½oz) plain flour
50g (1¾oz) ground almonds
double cream, to serve

**YOU WILL NEED**
20cm (8in) round springform
   cake tin, greased, base
   and sides lined with
   baking parchment

1   To start the cake, place the clementines in a saucepan and pour over enough water to cover. Bring the water to the boil and cook for 1½ hours, topping up with more water as necessary, until the clementines are very soft. Drain, discarding the cooking water, and leave the clementines to cool. Cut each clementine in half and remove any pips. Put the fruit into a food processor – skin and all – and blitz for roughly 2 minutes, until smooth.

2   Preheat the oven to 190°C (170°C fan/375°F/Gas 5).

3   Now make the crumble. Using your fingertips, rub both types of sugar and the orange zest together in a mixing bowl to release the essential oils into the sugar. Add the rest of the crumble ingredients and rub together with your fingertips until it forms a chunky, crumbly mixture. Tip the crumble into the base of the cake tin and press down with the back of a spoon into an even layer. Set aside.

4   Tip the puréed clementines into a large bowl with the rest of the cake ingredients and mix well to a batter. Pour the mixture into the cake tin, over the crumble base, and level the top with a palette knife. Bake for 1 hour, or until golden and a skewer inserted into the middle comes out clean. (Check the cake after 40 minutes and cover the top of the tin with foil if the cake is becoming too dark.)

5   Remove the cake from the oven, leave it in the tin, and place it on a wire rack to cool completely. Place a plate or cake stand on top of the tin and turn the cake over to release it from the tin. Remove the lining paper and serve cut into slices with cream on the side.

# Pear & Chocolate Upside Down Tart

This tart has everything I love about the indulgence of Christmas: a nutty, creamy frangipane; rich, intense chocolate; buttery, flaky puff pastry, and sweet, juicy pears. What could be more perfect for a Christmas dessert or celebratory tea?

## Serves 6–8

320g (11oz) sheet of ready-rolled puff pastry, roughly 35 x 23cm (14 x 9in), or use homemade (see p12)
1 tbsp melted butter
drizzle of runny honey
1 tbsp demerara sugar
3 just-ripe pears, peeled, halved lengthways, and cored, each half cut into 3 wedges
50g (1¾oz) plain chocolate, chopped
finely grated zest of ½ orange
1 egg, lightly beaten
icing sugar, for dusting

### For the frangipane:
120g (4¼oz) salted butter, softened
120g (4¼oz) caster sugar
2 large eggs, lightly beaten
120g (4¼oz) ground almonds
3 drops of almond extract

### YOU WILL NEED
large baking tray, roughly 38 x 27cm (15 x 10½in), lined with baking parchment
22cm (8½in) diameter round plate

1  Preheat the oven to 220°C (200°C fan/425°F/Gas 7). Unroll the sheet of pastry and cut out a round using the 22cm (8½in) diameter plate as a template. Place the pastry in the fridge until needed.

2  Draw around the same plate onto the baking parchment and place it drawn-side down on the baking tray. Set aside.

3  To make the frangipane, cream the butter and sugar in a large bowl using an electric hand whisk for 3 minutes, or until pale and fluffy. Add the eggs and half of the ground almonds, and beat again until combined. Mix in the almond extract and the remaining ground almonds, then set aside.

4  Brush the melted butter over the drawn round on the lined baking tray, then drizzle with a little honey. Sprinkle over the demerara sugar.

5  Leaving a 2cm (¾in) border, arrange the pears in a flower shape within the circle. Spoon over the frangipane and carefully spread it out evenly over the pears to cover. Scatter the chocolate and orange zest over the top.

6  Drape the pastry round over the pear and frangipane mixture. Using the back of a fork, press the edge of the pastry to seal. Score the top in a diamond pattern with a sharp knife and then brush with egg.

7  Bake for 30 minutes, until the pastry is golden and crisp. Remove the tart from the oven and allow it to sit on the tray for 10 minutes. Lay a piece of baking parchment on top, followed by a chopping board or plate, and carefully flip it over. Remove the tray and peel off the backing paper. Dust the top of the tart with icing sugar before serving.

# Sticky Toffee Christmas Pudding

We're not really Christmas pudding people in our house. For me, Christmas lunch is all about the incredible main course, and I'm always too full to eat anything other than a few sweets from a box of Roses. That said, if I'm craving dessert, this upside-down sticky toffee pudding is it; it's light but still has those indulgent Christmas pudding vibes, thanks to the warming spices and dried fruit. Plus, it is served with lashings of brandy toffee sauce.

## Serves 6–8

**For the pudding:**

125g (4½oz) dates, pitted and finely chopped
50g (1¾oz) mixed dried fruit and candied peel
100ml (3½fl oz) brandy
75g (2½oz) butter, softened
25g (scant 1oz) light muscovado sugar
2 eggs, lightly beaten
185g (6½oz) self-raising flour, sifted
large pinch of ground mixed spice
½ tsp ground cinnamon
1½ tbsp whole milk

**For the brandy toffee sauce:**

30g (1oz) light muscovado sugar
2 tbsp golden syrup
30g (1oz) salted butter
5 tbsp double cream, plus extra to serve
1½ tbsp brandy

**YOU WILL NEED**

1.5 litre (2¾ pint) pudding basin, greased generously with butter

1   Put the dates, mixed fruit, brandy, and 100ml (3½fl oz) water in a saucepan over a low heat (or do this in a microwave). Bring to a gentle simmer and cook for about 5 minutes, until the fruit has softened. Leave to cool.

2   Meanwhile, make the brandy toffee sauce. Place the muscovado sugar, golden syrup, and butter in a small saucepan. Bring to a simmer and cook for 5 minutes, until the sugar dissolves. Remove the pan from the heat and gently pour in the cream and brandy. Return the pan to a low heat and cook for a further 2 minutes, stirring continuously, then set aside.

3   To make the pudding, using an electric hand whisk, cream the butter and sugar in a large bowl until light and fluffy. (You can also do this in a stand mixer.) Add the eggs, flour, and ground spices and beat again until combined. Fold in the softened fruit and its liquid, then stir in the milk.

4   Pour a quarter of the brandy toffee sauce into the base of the prepared basin, then spoon in the pudding batter. Place a sheet of foil on top of a sheet of baking parchment (they should be large enough to cover the top of the pudding basin with some overhang), then make a pleat down the centre of both. Cover the pudding basin, baking parchment-side down, and tie it securely under the lip of the basin using kitchen string.

5   Transfer the basin to a steamer, cover, and cook over a low heat for 3 hours, checking the water level every so often and topping up when needed. Remove the paper and foil cover, then place a plate over the top of the pudding and flip it upside down out of the basin. Warm the remaining sauce, then pour it over the pudding before serving with cream.

# Cock
# &
# Can

# tails
# apés

My friend, Lisa, knows how to host a party. For her, It's not just about the food and drinks, the people, or even the location, it's about the joy you bring to it all. Everything you serve should be filled with fun, flavour, and colour, and that's the vibe I'm trying to bring in this chapter. Here, I've paired my favourite cocktails with small bites or canapés, incorporating flavours and styles that complement each other. That said, feel free to mix things up! Cocktails and canapés should make you think about parties and bringing people together to celebrate. Nothing should be too perfect, rather it should be an abundance of feasting joy.

# Upside Down Prawn Tostadas

The Viking and I had an incredible trip to Puerto Vallarta, Mexico, last spring. This spicy prawn canapé is inspired by a meal enjoyed on the beach there at sunset. Serve the upside-down mini tarts with my Marmalade Margarita (see p196) for the ultimate indulgent sundowner.

## Makes 6

### For the prawn tostadas:
320g (11oz) sheet of ready-rolled shortcrust pastry, roughly 35 x 23cm (14 x 9in), or use homemade (see p12)
2 tbsp chilli jam
200g (7oz) raw king prawns
2 garlic cloves, crushed
2 tsp chipotle (fajita) seasoning mix
2 shallots, cut into rings
1 egg, lightly beaten
salt and freshly ground black pepper

### For the grilled guacamole:
½ small red onion, sliced
2 fresh red chillies, halved lengthways and deseeded
2 avocados, peeled and sliced
2 tomatoes, cut in half
juice and grated zest of 2 limes
2 tbsp extra virgin olive oil, plus extra for drizzling
1 garlic clove, crushed
1 tsp chipotle (fajita) seasoning mix
1 handful of coriander leaves

### YOU WILL NEED
large baking tray, roughly 38 x 27cm (15 x 10½in), lined with baking parchment
9cm (3½in) cookie cutter

1. Preheat the oven to 220°C (200°C fan/425°F/Gas 7). Unroll the sheet of pastry and stamp out 6 rounds using the cookie cutter. Spread a teaspoon of chilli jam over one side of each round, leaving a narrow border around the edge. Place on a tray in the fridge until needed.

2. To make the grilled guacamole, put the onion in a large bowl with the chillies, avocados, and tomatoes. Add half of the lime juice, half of the olive oil, the garlic, and the spice mix. Mix gently until combined. Place a griddle pan on a medium heat. Lay the onion, chillies, avocados, and tomatoes in the hot pan and griddle until golden in places and softened slightly. Set aside to cool. When cool, roughly chop everything with some of the coriander leaves; you can go as small or chunky as you like. Place the guacamole in a bowl and season with salt. Stir in the rest of the lime juice and zest, and drizzle over some more olive oil. Set aside in the fridge while you make the tostadas.

3. Place the prawns in a large bowl with 1 tablespoon of olive oil, the garlic, and spice mix. Mix well and set aside.

4. Using the cutter as a template, draw 6 rounds onto the sheet of baking parchment, leaving space between each one, and place drawn-side down on the baking tray. Drizzle olive oil over the lined baking tray, then season with salt and pepper. Leaving a narrow border around the edge, scatter the shallot rings over each marked round. Top with the prawns, roughly 3 per tart, and spoon over the flavoured oil in the bowl.

5. Drape a pastry round, chilli jam-side down, over each pile of prawns. Using the back of a teaspoon, scallop the edge of each pastry round to seal. Score a cross on the top of the puffs with a sharp knife and then brush with egg.

6. Bake for 25 minutes, or until the pastry is golden and crisp. Remove the tostadas from the oven and allow them to sit on the tray for 5 minutes before flipping over. Top with the guacamole and coriander, then serve with a Marmalade Margarita.

# Antipasti Rolls

These are my new go-to canapés. The options for fillings are almost endless, but I'm showing you my favourite Italian-inspired one. You must trust the process here and work fast to roll up the pastry when it comes out of the oven. Even though they're utterly messy to eat, these divine bites are delicious, fun, and a little bit silly. A Lemon Cosmopolitan (see p199) is the perfect zingy partner.

**Makes about 18**

320g (11oz) sheet of ready-
    rolled puff pastry, roughly
    35 x 23cm (14 x 9in), or use
    homemade (see p12)
drizzle of olive oil
1 tsp chopped rosemary
1 tsp chopped thyme
1 egg, lightly beaten
150g (5½oz) Pesto (see p15)
    or use a shop-bought
    alternative
12 slices of prosciutto crudo
250g (9oz) mozzarella,
    drained, torn, or sliced
1 large bunch (30g/1oz)
    basil leaves
salt and freshly ground
    black pepper

**YOU WILL NEED**
large baking tray, roughly
    38 x 27cm (15 x 10½in),
    lined with baking parchment

1  Preheat the oven to 220°C (200°C fan/425°F/Gas 7). Unroll the sheet of pastry and set aside.

2  Drizzle olive oil over the lined baking tray and sprinkle with the rosemary and thyme. Season with salt and pepper.

3  Place the sheet of pastry on the lined baking tray. Score the top in a diamond pattern with a sharp knife and then brush with egg. Bake for 25 minutes, or until golden and crisp.

4  Meanwhile, prepare the rest of your ingredients so you're ready to go when the pastry comes out of the oven as you need to build the rolls while it is still warm.

5  Once the pastry is cooked and still warm, carefully place the baking tray on a flat surface and begin to layer the filling ingredients. Start by slathering the pastry all over with pesto, then top with a layer of prosciutto, then mozzarella, and finally the basil leaves. Season with salt and pepper, then cut the pastry in half horizontally (from long edge to long edge).

6  Deftly roll up one of the topped pastry sheets, starting from a short edge, until you have a large roll. Repeat with the second sheet, then cut both rolls into 2.5cm (1in) thick slices. Serve on a platter with a Lemon Cosmopolitan.

# Roast Tomato, Garlic & Mozzarella Sharing Platter

This sharing plate of roasted garlic and tomato-topped toasts, with the addition of mozzarella and fresh basil, is one of the messiest things to eat, but if the truth be told, that adds to its appeal. Originated by my friend, Lisa, the platter makes a phenomenal dish at a party, barbecue, or picnic – everyone just dives in and gets messy with it – especially with a glass or two of my Roast Tomato Bloody Mary (see p199).

## Serves 6–8

3 punnets of small vine
  tomatoes (try and find a
  mix of sizes and colours,
  if possible)
1 large garlic bulb
4 tbsp extra virgin olive oil,
  plus extra to drizzle
4 tbsp balsamic vinegar
1 tsp dried oregano
1 generous handful of
  basil leaves
salt and freshly ground
  black pepper

**To serve:**
1 long baguette or 4 ciabatta
1 punnet of cherry tomatoes,
  cut in half
3 x 125g (4½oz) balls of
  mozzarella, drained and
  torn into pieces

**YOU WILL NEED**
large roasting tin

1 Preheat the oven to 200°C (180°C fan/400°F/Gas 6). Place the small vine tomatoes in a large roasting tin. Break the garlic bulb apart and scatter the cloves (still in their skins) around the tomatoes. Spoon over the olive oil and balsamic vinegar. Season with oregano, salt, and pepper, then add the basil leaves (saving some to serve). Roast in the oven for roughly 30 minutes, until the tomatoes are soft and beginning to burst, and the garlic cloves are tender. Turn off the heat but leave the tray inside the oven to allow the tomatoes to cool slowly.

2 Thickly slice the bread and drizzle both sides with olive oil. Place a griddle pan on a high heat and griddle the bread on both sides until crisp and slightly blackened in places. Arrange the bread on a large chopping board or platter.

3 Remove the cooled roasted garlic and tomatoes from the oven. Squeeze the garlic cloves out of their skins onto the griddled bread and spread it out with the back of a spoon. Lay the roasted tomatoes on top of the garlic and squish them down slightly with the back of the spoon.

4 To serve, scatter the fresh tomatoes and mozzarella over the toasts. Season with salt and pepper, then scatter over some basil leaves. Drizzle generously with extra olive oil. Serve with a Roast Tomato Bloody Mary.

# Upside Down Cherry & Feta Bites

I love a little treat I can pop into my mouth while cooking or waiting for guests to arrive, or to enjoy with a cocktail. Not that I need an excuse to nibble on these sweet-but-savoury little bites. The juiciness of the cherries works well with the savoury, salty feta, and they are perfect bedfellows with my ridiculously drinkable Blender Amaretto Sour (see p196).

## Makes 16

320g (11oz) sheet of ready-
  rolled shortcrust pastry,
  roughly 35 x 23cm
  (14 x 9in), or use
  homemade (see p12)
drizzle of olive oil
1 tsp chopped thyme leaves,
  plus extra to garnish
1 egg, lightly beaten

### For the filling:
250g (9oz) cherries, pitted
1 courgette, chopped
1 tbsp chopped dill
½ tbsp chopped mint leaves
200g (7oz) feta, crumbled
50g (1¾oz) unsalted,
  shelled pistachios
1 egg
salt and freshly ground
  black pepper

### YOU WILL NEED
large baking tray, roughly
  38 x 27cm (15 x 10½in),
  lined with baking parchment
5.5cm (2¼in) cookie cutter

1   Preheat the oven to 220°C (200°C fan/425°F/Gas 7). Unroll the sheet of pastry and stamp out 16 rounds using the cookie cutter. Place on a tray in the fridge until needed.

2   Place all the ingredients for the filling in a food processor (reserving 16 cherries and a third of the feta for later) and blend to a rough paste. Season with salt and pepper, then set aside

3   Drizzle olive oil over the lined baking tray and sprinkle with thyme. Season with salt and pepper. Arrange 16 cherries (in 4 rows of 4), evenly spaced apart, on the lined tray.

4   Remove the pastry discs from the fridge and spread a teaspoon of the filling over the top of each one, leaving a narrow border around the edge.

5   Drape a pastry round filling-side down over the cherries. Using the back of a fork, press around the edge of the pastry rounds to seal. Score a cross on top of each one with a sharp knife and then brush with egg.

6   Bake for 25 minutes, or until golden and crisp. Remove the tarts from the oven and allow them to sit on the tray for 5 minutes. Slide a spatula underneath each one and deftly flip them over onto a serving platter. Scatter over a little extra thyme and the reserved crumbled feta. Serve with a Blender Amaretto Sour. Cin cin.

# Upside Down Chilli Chutney Cauliflower Tarts

Cauliflower is such a versatile vegetable. If cooked correctly, it holds its shape and texture, without turning mushy, which is great for these mini tarts. It also readily absorbs flavourings, such as this lime and chilli chutney. Any flavour will work, so choose your favourite and have fun with it. The tarts are perfect with a glass or two of my Rumdelion cocktail (see p199).

## Makes 6

320g (11oz) sheet of ready-
   rolled puff pastry, roughly
   35 x 23cm (14 x 9in), or use
   homemade (see p12)
6 tsp lime and chilli chutney
drizzle of chilli oil
6 cauliflower florets
drizzle of olive oil
1 egg, lightly beaten
salt and freshly ground
   black pepper

**YOU WILL NEED**
large baking tray, roughly
   38 x 27cm (15 x 10½in),
   lined with baking parchment

1   Preheat the oven to 220°C (200°C fan/425°F/Gas 7). Unroll the sheet of pastry and cut it into 6 even-sized squares, each about 11 x 11cm (4½ x 4½in). Spread 1 teaspoon of chutney over the middle of each square, leaving a wide border. Place on a tray in the fridge until needed.

2   Mark out 6 squares on the baking parchment, the same size as the pastry and with space between each one, then place the paper drawn-side down on the baking tray. Drizzle with the chilli oil, then season with salt and pepper. Place a cauliflower floret in the centre of each square and drizzle over some olive oil.

3   Drape a square of pastry, chutney-side down, over each floret. Using the back of a teaspoon, scallop the edge of each pastry square to seal. Score the top of the tarts in a diamond pattern with a sharp knife and then brush with egg.

4   Bake for 25 minutes, until golden and crisp. Remove the tarts from the oven and allow them to sit on the tray for 5 minutes. Slide a spatula underneath each one and deftly flip them over onto a serving platter. Serve with The Rumdelion cocktail.

# The Art of Making Cocktails

**When it comes to making cocktails, it's all about simplicity, speed, and just a little drama.**

Preparation is key, and while I think a jug suits certain cocktails (and you should definitely own one!), the spectacle of shaking a cocktail or two is always something special. To keep the cocktails flowing, I have a few simple tips, beginning with an absolute must: a cocktail station. I suggest stocking it with the following:

- Large ice bucket, always filled with ice (you can never have enough ice)
- Selection of cut citrus fruits (lime, lemon, and orange slices or wedges)
- Selection of large jugs and stirrers
- Collection of cocktail shakers (one is never enough)
- Selection of glassware: highballs, shorts, wine glasses, and Martini-style glasses
- Salt or sugar in saucers, to add to the rims of your cocktail glasses
- No straws (straws are for children and just get in the way)
- Large high-speed blender (that can cope with ice)
- A friend who is happy to be the cocktail waiter for the evening.

# Cocktail Time

I adore making cocktails but they must be quick and simple as well as convey an air of sophistication. On the following pages, I have included a few of my favourites, which all partner beautifully with the canapés in this chapter. Before you start, I recommend you have the prepared ingredients to hand and measured out, and to keep the cocktails flowing, I suggest a few essentials kitchen items (see p194 for my full list).

## Marmalade Margarita

**MAKES 2** *(pictured on p184)*

This is a cute little twist on the classic margarita, made with the last scrapings in the bottom of a marmalade jar. I make the cocktail in the jar, which helps to loosen the residual marmalade and adds to the flavour.

### INGREDIENTS
juice and finely grated zest of ½ orange
large handful of sea salt
ice
2 tbsp marmalade (any kind will work)
100ml (3½fl oz) tequila
50ml (1¾fl oz) fresh lime juice
50ml (1¾fl oz) triple sec

### YOU WILL NEED
marmalade jar (near empty) or cocktail shaker

1   To start, decorate the rims of 2 martini glasses. Squeeze the orange juice into a shallow bowl and put the grated orange zest in a saucer. Add the salt to the zest and mix until combined. Dip the rims of the glasses into the orange juice, then into the orange zest-salt mix until coated. Set aside.

2   Add some ice to the marmalade jar containing 2 tablespoons of marmalade. Pour in the tequila, lime juice, and triple sec, then close the lid and shake well. If you don't have a near-empty marmalade jar, then add the ingredients to a cocktail shaker along with 2 tablespoons of marmalade and shake. Pour into the prepared glasses and enjoy.

## Blender Amaretto Sour

**MAKES 4** *(pictured right)*

I adore a sour cocktail; it appeals to my love of anything sherbetty and sweet-sharp. I also like cherries and almonds, so think of this cocktail as a cherry Bakewell tart in a glass, which is just as heavenly, and slightly deadly, as it sounds.

### INGREDIENTS
400ml (14fl oz) amaretto
juice of 4–6 lemons (you need 240ml/8fl oz)
2 egg whites
350g (12oz) jar of (pitted) Opies black
    cherries in kirsch
ice

### YOU WILL NEED
high-speed blender (one that can cope with ice)

1   Put the amaretto, lemon juice, egg whites, and 3 tablespoons of the kirsch from the jar into a blender. Add 5 cherries and a handful of ice. Whizz on high speed until pale and frothy, and starting to increase in volume.

2   Pour the cocktail into rock glasses or tumblers and decorate with a cherry to serve.

## The Rumdelion

**MAKES 1** *(pictured left)*

They say that out of necessity comes invention, and this fabulous cocktail was invented by my husband, The Viking, during the COVID pandemic of 2020, when going to a bar wasn't an option. For those unfamiliar with Dandelion and Burdock, it has a wonderful flavour, with hints of liquorice and vanilla, but if you can't find it, the best alternative is root beer or Dr Pepper.

### INGREDIENTS

ice
50ml (1¾fl oz) dark spiced rum (our
  preference would be Kraken)
150ml (5½fl oz) Dandelion and Burdock

1   Fill a highball glass with ice. Add the rum and top up with Dandelion and Burdock. Stir.

## Lemon Cosmopolitan

**MAKES 1** *(pictured on p187)*

Mum and I have many things in common – our love of cakes, fish and chips, and having a good laugh spring to mind – but one of the best things I share with her is our love of a cosmopolitan. It's our go-to drink at any bar or party. This is a lemony twist on my favourite. It's one for the shaker, but it's so easy it can be made on repeat.

### INGREDIENTS

45ml (3 tbsp) lemon vodka
15ml (1 tbsp) triple sec
30ml (2 tbsp) cranberry juice
10ml (2 tsp) lime juice
ice

### To serve

3cm (1¼in) strip of orange peel

### YOU WILL NEED

cocktail shaker

1   Put all the ingredients into a cocktail shaker, shake, and strain into a cocktail glass. Hold the orange zest about 10cm (4in) above your cosmo and very carefully wave it over a lit match or lighter flame. Bend the outer edge of the zest in towards the flame to release the orange oils, then add to your cocktail.

## Roast Tomato Bloody Mary

**MAKES 6** *(pictured on p189)*

This takes a regular bloody Mary to another level. As for its reputation for curing a hangover, I'm not entirely sure, I'd probably consider it just an excuse to enjoy a cocktail – it's certainly moreish.

### INGREDIENTS

750ml (1¼ pints) tomato juice
300ml (10fl oz) vodka
ice, lemon slices, celery sticks, and
  Tabasco, to finish

### For the roasted tomatoes:

800g (1¾lb) vine cherry tomatoes
splash of balsamic vinegar
2 tbsp olive oil
1 tbsp Worcestershire sauce
1 tsp chilli flakes
1 tsp celery salt
3 garlic cloves
1 lemon, cut into wedges
salt and freshly ground black pepper

### YOU WILL NEED

large roasting tin
high-speed blender

1   Preheat the oven to 180°C (160°C fan/ 350°F/Gas 4). Place all the ingredients for the roasted tomatoes in a large roasting tin. Season and mix well. Roast for 30 minutes, until the tomatoes are soft, then remove from the oven and leave to cool.

2   Discard the lemon wedges, then tip everything into a blender. Blitz until smooth, then pour in the tomato juice and vodka, and blend again briefly. Pour into a jug, and add ice and lemon slices. Serve in highball glasses with more ice, a stick of celery, and a dash of Tabasco.

# Index

# About the Author

**Dominic Franks** is a food writer and home cook who takes inspiration from Delia Smith, his Mum, his Jewish heritage, and his London upbringing. He lives in Lincolnshire with his husband, Andy, where he has been cooking and writing for his food blog *Dom in the Kitchen* since 2010. He writes for *Lincolnshire Life Magazine* and is regularly featured on *BBC Radio Lincolnshire* as their food expert.

You can follow Dom on Instagram at **@dominthekitchen** and find more of Dom's recipes at **dominthekitchen.com**

# Acknowledgments

I'd like to dedicate this book to Kyra. If I didn't, she would probably stop talking to me, and I'm hoping this goes at least a small way to repairing her omission from my first book, *Upside Down Cooking*.

I feel unbelievably honoured that the team at DK had the confidence and faith in me to commission a second book. I'd very much like to start by thanking them and for guiding me through the process so smoothly. I've enjoyed every minute of it, perhaps even more so than the first book as I've been able to step back and relish the process, rather than feel like a deer caught in the headlights as I sometimes did with my first one. I'd like to thank Cara, Lucy, and Tania for being so brilliant, plus Cora and Silvia, who did such a tremendous job marketing *Upside Down Cooking*. My editor, Nicola, just makes the whole process so easy and continues to understand my quirks.

To any budding cookbook writer out there, my main piece of advice would be to get yourself a literary agent like Liza. Thank you for always being there for me.

Thank you to Ellis Parrinder, Susanna Unsworth, and Max Robinson my photographer, food stylist, and stylist, who helped me create the unique vision for this book and for always being willing to take it to the next step.

Thank you again to Pauline at Nordic Ware for always being so supportive and generous with the supply of their amazing baking sheets and cake tins.

Thank you to Mum and Eric, and Dad and Jette – double the family, double the inspiration. As well as being a confidant, Mum can always be relied on for a hand- me-down recipe and a little mum wisdom when trying out new recipes. Dad is a secret keeper of family memories and many of them involve food, so he's always great to rely on for a bit of cookery retrospection. While the initial trauma of parental divorce can sting, a few decades on, my parents' spouses (or bonus mum and dad as we call them) have also become a well of recipe inspiration, for which I am grateful.

I'd like to thank Lisa, who once again gives the best advice and reminds me regularly to breathe, take it all in and enjoy the process.

And, of course, to all my friends, I promise I'll call you, once you call me to let me know you've purchased this book! I'd like to extend a special thanks to Jenny and Phillipa, who have been so supportive and allowed me to be frivolous while they work so hard.

Again, I want to thank all my wonderful social media family. Thanks for the follows, likes, shares, and comments. It's a community that I treasure with all my heart. Thank you to Dawny, who works tirelessly behind the scenes.

And finally, to my husband, best friend, and constant companion, Andy (The Viking). Thank you for being here by my side. You are my everything.

**Publisher's Acknowledgments**
DK would like to thank John Friend for proofreading and Lisa Footitt for providing the index.

**DK LONDON**
**Editorial Director** Cara Armstrong
**Senior Editor** Lucy Sienkowska
**Design Manager** Tania Gomes
**DTP and Design Coordinator** Heather Blagden
**Production Editor** Becky Fallowfield
**Senior Production Controller** Stephanie McConnell
**Art Director** Maxine Pedliham
**Publishing Director** Stephanie Jackson

**Editorial** Nicola Graimes
**Design** Amy Child
**Design Development** Studio Nic & Lou
**Photography** Ellis Parrinder
**Food Styling** Susanna Unsworth and Kristine Jakobsson
**Prop Styling** Max Robinson

First published in Great Britain in 2026 by
Dorling Kindersley Limited
20 Vauxhall Bridge Road,
London SW1V 2SA

The authorised representative in the EEA is
Dorling Kindersley Verlag GmbH. Arnulfstr. 124,
80636 Munich, Germany

A CIP catalogue record for this book
is available from the British Library.
ISBN: 978-0-2417-3228-1

Printed and bound in China
**www.dk.com**

This book was made with Forest
Stewardship Council™ certified
paper – one small step in DK's
commitment to a sustainable future.
Learn more at
**www.dk.com/uk/information/sustainability**